HADRIAN'S WALL

Hadrian's Wall

A Social and Cultural History

Alison Ewin

Centre for North-West Regional Studies
University of Lancaster
2000
Title Editor: David Shotter
Series Editor: Jean Turnbull

Hadrian's Wall

This volume is the 41st in a series published by the Centre for North-West Regional Studies at the University of Lancaster

Text copyright © Alison Ewin 2000

Published by the Centre for North-West Regional Studies, University of Lancaster

Designed and typeset by Carnegie Publishing Ltd, Carnegie House, Chatsworth Road, Lancaster LA1 4SL

Printed and bound in the UK by Cromwell Press, Trowbridge

British Library Cataloguing-in-Publication Data
A CIP catalogue record for this book is available from the British Library

ISBN 1–86220-096-3

Contents

Foreword

Designated as a World Heritage Site, Hadrian's Wall attracts large number of visitors; nearly half-a-million people visited specific sites in 1999, and the overall number of those visiting in less formal ways must at least double that figure. A far cry from the situation in the nineteenth century, when sites were owned by privileged individuals, such as John Clayton, who could use them for their own research – and for the pleasure of themselves and of their friends.

The birth of the 'learned Societies' in the nineteenth century certainly served to expand accessibility from then into the earlier years of the twentieth, under the 'banners' of men such as Collingwood Bruce, the Collingwoods and the late Eric Birley. But even in the early days there were a few, such as Robert Blair of South Shields and his colleagues on the local Council, who looked to widen accessibility for *ordinary* people.

Alison Ewin's book is *not* 'yet another publication on Hadrian's Wall'; it started life as a thesis for a Master's Degree in History at Lancaster University, and provides a social study of the changing patterns of interest in and access to this great monument, and of the provision of material to inform and educate visitors whose age-range has changed as dramatically as their class-range.

It is particularly fitting that this book should be published now – just after the twelfth of the traditional 'pilgrimages' (held in 1999) which began in the nineteenth century; it also comes at a time when strenuous steps are being taken to open up access still further, through reconstructions, such as the gateway at South Shields and the bath-house at Wallsend, and through such exciting ventures as the creation of a 'Heritage Trail' along the length of the Wall. Throughout, the book is illustrated by drawings and photographs, much of which is archive-material, which serve, along with Alison Ewin's text, to recapture atmosphere and pre-occupations, both old and new, and to demonstrate how different a matter Hadrian's Wall is in 2000 compared with 1900 – and still more with 1800.

David Shotter

Acknowledgements

This book owes much to those who helped with the dissertation upon which it is based and in the changes required to bring it to publication. I am particularly grateful to Dr David Shotter of the Department of History at Lancaster University who supervised the dissertation and has played an invaluable role as editor of the book. Also to Lindsay Allason-Jones of the Department of Archaeology at the University of Newcastle upon Tyne and Georgina Plowright, Curator of the Museums at Housesteads, Chesters and Corbridge for their advice and guidance. Finally, I would like to thank my colleagues at St Martin's College, Cliff O'Neill and Ian Phillips, for their encouragement and support.

The illustrations reproduced in this book are an important part of the whole. I am grateful to those organisations and individuals who have given permission for the use of particular images. They include: the Museum of Antiquities of the University and Society of Antiquaries of Newcastle upon Tyne; the Northumberland Record Office; English Heritage; the Corbridge Excavation Fund and publisher Frank Graham. I would like to offer special thanks to B. J. N. Edwards, Ian Caruana of the Cumberland and Westmorland Antiquarian and Archaeological Society, Dr L. M. Newman of Lancaster University Library and the Photographic Unit at Lancaster University, all of whom helped by locating and reproducing images for the book.

List of Illustrations

CHAPTER ONE

Introduction

In 1987 UNESCO announced a list of World Heritage Sites which included Hadrian's Wall. This designation recognises the unique nature of this monument which is 'one of the most significant complexes of archaeological remains of any period in the world'.[1] It has been the focus of both scholarly research and popular interest for at least three hundred years. In that time, it has been visited, studied, recorded, excavated, painted, photographed, legislated for, argued over and for some it has become their life's work. It is the largest monument in Britain and one of the most significant in its rarity and complexity. There are Roman frontier works in other parts of what was once the Roman Empire but none are as concentrated, as extensively researched or as well preserved as Hadrian's Wall and its associated military zone.

The dictates of geography and geology have helped create a structure that is difficult to ignore. Its location, perched on the Whin Sill and running from the Tyne to the Solway, together with its complex mix of earth-works and stone structures have combined to produce an enigma that continues to evade the precise definitions and labels historians and archaeologists often seek to attach to such remains. It is only comparatively recently that Hadrian's name has been attached to the Wall. Early designations simply referred to the 'Roman Wall'. In the absence of any precise documentary context for its origins, its complexity has resulted in a wealth of often conflicting interpretations and consequently a long historiography.

From its inception early in the second century AD, it must have been an object of admiration. The contemporary *Rudge Cup*, which bears an image of the Wall and the names of forts along its length, must be one of the first recorded souvenirs of any monument in Britain. The first written account since the Roman period comes from Bede who in his *Ecclesiastical History* describes the Wall as it was in the eighth century: 'This wall, a famous landmark to this day, ... is eight feet wide and twelve feet high, and runs in a straight line from east to west, as can be clearly seen today'. The first account of any length is contained in William Camden's *Britannia* which first appeared in 1586. From this point it is possible to delineate a strand of historical research running through to the present day. The evolution of archaeology as a recognised discipline is intimately connected with research on the Wall in the nineteenth and twentieth centuries. Britain was in the forefront of the development of a methodology for archaeology and, as an imperial power, was able to gain access to and excavate in many parts of the world. The Wall was the training ground for many of those who later gained international reputations and its study remains a major feature of the current British archaeological scene.

The Wall is, however, much more than the object of academic research. It is a monument with all that that entails. The root of the word is the Latin *monere* (to remind). It therefore has connotations of empathy with a past which entails an emotional response as well as scholarly interest. It is the totality of this response that this book seeks to explore. The interaction between people and a relic set in a certain landscape is the product of a vast number of influences – social, cultural and psychological. For example, the British scholar of the nineteenth century would have had a predisposition to identify with all things Roman. Many of the references in this book point to the Roman Empire as a model of what an empire ought to be; a consideration of great contemporary importance when Britain was herself in control of a third of the world and seeking to create the imagery to accompany the fact. Classical learning was still the core of a gentleman's education and the foundation of university courses. The problem of the Empire's decadence and subsequent decline and the Victorian admiration for the Anglo-Saxons as a supposedly freedom-loving people created much ambiguity in Victorian attitudes. For the visitors to the Wall, there were other preconceptions. The Romantic movement often broods over visitors' descriptions of the remains. The idea of the Wall as a frontier and therefore by definition a linear monument reinforced ideas of journeys and pilgrimages.

Much of the nineteenth- and early twentieth-century history of the Wall tends to concern itself with a narrow social stratum as regards both visitors and researchers. The democratisation of the interaction between the two is intimately connected with the rise of mass tourism. Archaeology's exponents had to develop a different relationship with a public with new expectations and perceptions and the impact this has had on the structure itself has been profound. The two themes of conservation and interpretation underlie this evolution and, though their roots are to be found in the nineteenth century, their importance gradually increases through the twentieth. In particular the 'green consciousness' movement has reinforced the idea that fragility is a feature of the modern man-made world as well as of the natural world.

The idea of an ancient monument as an aspect of a nation's 'heritage' is vital to any discussion of the fate of an archaeological site. Hadrian's Wall has a significance much greater than the sum of its parts. As a cultural resource, as a symbol of Roman power and influence there is now a general acceptance that it should be preserved. This has not always been the case and a study of the evolution of this idea reveals great ambiguity about where the responsibility for preservation lies. In a modern democratic society the guardianship of the nation's heritage should perhaps lie with its government: this, however, presupposes that public perceptions of for whom and what the monument exists coincide with those of the state and its bureaucracy. The 'public' itself is unlikely to agree on its needs, some seeing the Wall in historical terms, others valuing it for its beautiful scenery, some wanting to see it reconstructed, others valuing it as a romantic ruin. The relationship between public and private enterprise is a consistent theme of this study.

It is hoped that such contemporary issues will be elucidated by looking at the history of the Wall in social and cultural terms from the points of view both of individuals and of their institutions. Chronologically, the emphasis of the book is on the last two centuries, being the period during which the monument was, in a sense, physically created. In other words, this was the period when the Wall was consciously excavated, preserved and recorded. The resulting structure has been visited by vast numbers of people with vastly differing motives. Their perceptions are the building blocks of this monument as much as the stones and mortar initially aligned from sea to sea nearly two thousand years ago.

Notes on the Bibliography

The history of a monument is an amalgam of various other histories. Firstly, there is the historiography of the research of the monument, of its contribution to a scholarly understanding of the Roman history of Britain and of the Empire as a whole. This research has a wide literature in the form of books, journals and conference papers. Mural studies have attracted some of the great names of Roman history and archaeology; R. G. Collingwood was the first to attempt a model for the historiography of research on the Wall. In 1923 he published a paper entitled, *Hadrian's Wall: a History of the Problem*.[2] An advocate of an empirical approach to archaeology, his main concern here was an analysis of the changing questions being asked about the nature and purpose of the Wall in the light of excavation. After Collingwood the historiography of the Wall is dominated by one man, Eric Birley. His *Research on Hadrian's Wall*[3] was written in 1961 and is now out of print. Birley held the chair of Archaeology at Durham University and was probably the most experienced of all scholars of the Wall. The book is a handbook covering all aspects of research from Bede to the excavations of the immediate post-war period. It catalogues all the primary and secondary sources known to the author detailing them site by site. It follows in Collingwood's tradition in that it concentrates on the contribution of research to the 'problem' of the interpretation of the Wall, its chronology, mode of construction, and function. It also alludes to the personalities and institutions involved in the research but recognises that these topics require more thorough study. 'The antiquarians and their contributions to knowledge of the Wall throw much incidental light on the social and intellectual history of the north of England.'[4] Chapter Two takes this observation to heart but reverses this statement by looking at the light shed on the monument by a study of the history of the social and intellectual life of Newcastle upon Tyne in particular. This book does not follow in Birley's footsteps in that it is not attempting to chronicle the academic research of the Wall.

The second history is that of the discipline of archaeology as a whole and this has been approached by archaeologists rather than historians. The principal authority is Stuart Piggott whose collection of essays *Ruins in a Landscape* of 1976 has been particularly influential in assessing the contribution of the Romantic movement to nineteenth-century attitudes to Antiquity. Glyn Daniel's survey of *150 Years of Archaeology*[5] remains the classic work on the subject but, being published in 1975, is rather out of date. It addresses the evolution of the discipline in its methodology and ideas rather than in its social and institutional context. Kenneth Hudson has published a *Social History of Archaeology*.[6] A profound and scholarly work is Philippa Levine's *The Amateur and the Professional*[7] which looks at the transition from antiquarian to professional archaeology on a nationwide scale. Chapter Two attempts to apply her thesis as it relates to a local situation.

A social history of Hadrian's Wall has not previously been attempted. Stephen Johnson's book for English Heritage[8] is largely an interpretation of the sites in their Roman context for visitors though his final two chapters discuss the archaeology and raise issues of conservation. Jim Crow's book in the same series on *Housesteads*[9] again concentrates on Roman history; however, his final chapters on the history of the excavations at Housesteads are well documented and use photographs and primary sources drawn from Newcastle University's Hadrian's Wall archive which is also used in this study.

The social and cultural history of another ancient monument for use as a potential model for this study was difficult to find: however there is Christopher Chippindale's *Stonehenge Complete*[10] which is an imaginative and witty look at Britain's most famous ancient monument in which he has 'tried to include everything important, interesting, or odd that has been written or painted, discovered or felt about the most extraordinary of all ancient buildings.'[11] This is large and lavishly illustrated, well beyond the scope of the present work. However, *Hadrian's Wall Complete* might be a worthy project for the future.

Hadrian's Wall has a vast and scattered archive of primary sources. To 1960 it has been partially catalogued by Eric Birley in *Research on Hadrian's Wall* but only in the context of books, research papers, reports and other documents. Archives relevant to Housesteads have been catalogued by Jim Crow for English Heritage and this has helped identify sources relating to other Wall sites.

Visually, the Wall has been extensively documented. There exists a rich resource of photographs, drawings and paintings, although they are nowhere comprehensively catalogued and are haphazardly located. This book has purposely drawn on visual sources wherever possible in the belief that people's most immediate response to such a monument is a visual one and this deserves careful analysis.

In studying the concerns of local archaeology the journals of the antiquarian societies have provided a fertile resource. Their transactions and proceedings have been of particular interest in that they provide a vivid insight into the social as well as the learned background to Wall archaeology. For the early period they are indispensable and would merit further detailed study than the constraints of this work allow. Later records of meetings become terse to the point of oblivion and the newsletters which have replaced the journals are unfortunately more ephemeral and no longer collected as a documentary record by libraries. For the modern period, newspaper accounts have been the principal source of information being particularly relevant to a study seeking to view archaeology from a popular viewpoint.

Documentation associated with tourism is not, by its nature, durable. The collection of the Museum of Antiquities at Newcastle University includes guidebooks, reports, and an assortment of ephemera of great interest though not systematically collected. The Museum library has also provided a number of examples of tourist literature from the early part of the century which, again, are only a small part of the likely available literature and are not necessarily representative but are a fascinating starting point for possible further study.

The structure of this book is thematic rather than chronological. The publication of the *Draft Management Plan for the Hadrian's Wall Military Zone* in August 1995 provides a framework for a critical discussion of the major themes implicit in the concept of a World Heritage Site and it has been the intention here to cast light on present issues by analysing them in historical terms. The main themes include the relationship between the needs and attitudes of scholars of the Wall and those of the visitors to the monument, the contribution made by public as opposed to private enterprise to the development of the Wall and, underlying all this, an analysis of the different meanings accruing to the Wall in its context as an ancient monument.

Notes

1. English Heritage, *Draft Management Plan, Hadrian's Wall Military Zone*, 1995, p. 7.
2. R. G. Collingwood, Hadrian's Wall: A History of the Problem, *Journal of Roman Studies*, XI (1921), p. 37.
3. E. Birley, *Research on Hadrian's Wall*, Kendal (1961).
4. *Ibid.*, p. 24.
5. G. Daniels, *150 Years of Archaeology*, London (1975).
6. K. Hudson, *A Social History of Archaeology*, London (1981).
7. P. Levine, *The Amateur and the Professional*, Cambridge (1986).
8. S. Johnson, *Hadrian's Wall*, London (1989).
9. J. Crow, *Housesteads*, London (1995).
10. C. Chippindale, *Stonehenge Complete*, London (1983).
11. *Ibid.*, p. 6.

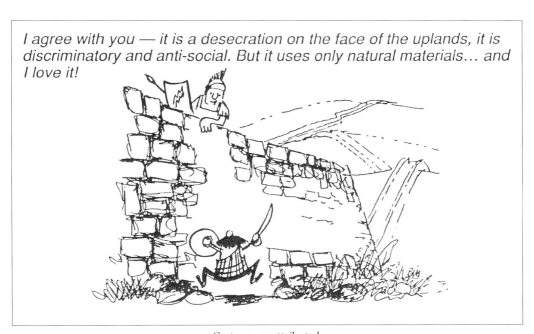

Cartoon, unattributed.

The Wall at Crag Lough. J. C. Bruce, *The Roman Wall*, 1853.

CHAPTER TWO

Early Institutions:
Amateurs and Professionals

Describing someone or something today as 'antiquarian' has pejorative undertones. It implies an unscientific, pettifogging approach to the past, an obsession with the collecting of objects for their own sake. In the nineteenth century the study of antiquities was generally considered a worthy leisure pursuit for men of talent and prestige. The evolution of antiquarianism into the modern discipline of archaeology is usefully exemplified by a study of the changing attitudes to Hadrian's Wall from the nineteenth into the twentieth century. The course of archaeological research on the Wall may be charted from its role as an off-shoot of early antiquarianism to becoming part of a recognised and coherent discipline with its own methodology, organisational and management structures. This evolution is characterised by a gradual change in the nature and origins of the prime movers in mural research. The idea of the academically motivated and trained practitioner arose between the Wars and this has had widespread repercussions on the approaches taken to research on the Wall and to the roles of the people taking part. The balance between the amateur and the professional has continued to be an underlying theme of the social history of archaeology to the present day. It is one that is often controversial and has impacted on the excavation of many Wall sites.

The origins of the relationship between amateurs and professionals needs to be understood in the context of other aspects of the intellectual life and associated social conditions and attitudes current at the time. A crucial aspect of any such understanding is an assessment of the contribution made by the antiquarian societies of the nineteenth century. These antiquarian societies originated in the eighteenth century, had their heyday in the nineteenth and are still of relevance today. They provided the focus and justification for those with the leisure, aptitude and money to indulge a curiosity about the physical remains of the past evident in their particular locality. These societies need therefore to be seen essentially as a provincial phenomenon though part of a network covering both Britain and, to a lesser degree, Europe.

The two societies of relevance to this study are the Society of Antiquaries of Newcastle upon Tyne and the Cumberland and West-morland Antiquarian and Archaeological Society, located, as might be expected, at the two centres of population at either end of the Wall. The Newcastle Society, founded in 1813, was the larger and senior institution. The Cumberland Society was founded in 1866. Emphasis is placed in this chapter on the development of the Newcastle Society although much that is stated is relevant to both societies, an element of their membership being always common to both.

The Newcastle Society formed part of a web of geological, literary, natural history and architectural societies, woven often by the same civic spiders prominent in the commerce, industry and govern-ment and also religious life of northern England's newly expanding cities. The individualism of the aristocratic collector of curiosities or the eccentric topographical observer and recorder such as William Stukeley was giving way to a group mentality which was such a notable feature of Victorian social and intellectual life. Early archae-ology's devotees were 'a highly motivated elite on familiar and friendly terms with one another and sharing a common body of knowledge'.[1] This does not mean, however, that the mid-century antiquarian scene lacked its personalities and, indeed, eccentrics.

A study of the membership of the Newcastle Society, founded in 1813, which makes it one of the elder-statesmen of such societies, illustrates some of the above generalisations. In 1913 the Society published a 'Centenary Volume' of its journal, *Archaeologia Aeliana*, in which there appeared a series of approximately ninety bio-graphies, plus portraits, of past contributors to the Society's literature. The series gives an interesting overview of the occupations and education of the Society's, by definition, most active members. Apart from a scattering of aristocratic, landowning patrons includ-ing the Dukes of Northumberland, MPs, and Justices, two of the traditional professions, the Law and the Church, predominate. Medicine is less well represented. Newer professions including archi-tecture, engineering and journalism are also in evidence. Business and commerce include leading ship-owners, brewers, coal-owners, and builders though these are small in number. Newcastle, in this period, established itself as one of Britain's major industrial cities. The redevelopment of the city's infrastructure and extensions of its city centre effectively turned it into the 'Metropolis of the North' by the 1840s and the intellectual life of the city was also led by those most intimately involved in this rapid expansion, the architects, lawyers, financiers and businessmen. What is reflected here is, therefore, a microcosm of influential society in nineteenth-century Newcastle. George Jobey surveyed the membership on the occasion of the Society's 175th anniversary and came to the conclusion that 'after the middle of the nineteenth century, the commercial, industrial and the science history of the North East, if not at times the nation, could well be written around the names of the many men of stature and some financial substance in these fields who were members of the Society'.[2]

The Newcastle Society, thus constituted, was an institution of great influence both in the development of scholarly research and the development of public awareness and interest in archaeology. Its concern was with, as it states in its constitution, 'antiquities in general'; however, any survey of the contents of *Archaeologia Aeliana*, gives an immediate indication of the primacy of the part played by the study of Roman remains. The Society's effectiveness as mediator between public and private interests in this area rested in its organisational capacity. As an institution, it was able to promote research and record the results in its journals, organise meetings of members as a forum for the discussion of the research, raise money by subscription to further research, establish museums to house the end products of the research and run field trips and other social events to visit the *in situ* evidence of the research. Proselytisation by public lecture raised further money.

As an institution, however, it was, of course, very much dependent for its success on the abilities of its members. To illustrate the theme of private, scholarly pursuit as against the promotion of public awareness it is worth studying two of the leading personalities of the society's nineteenth-century history. The private face of Roman antiquarianism is undoubtedly represented by John Clayton, the public by John Collingwood Bruce. John Clayton's life, his background, education, and approach to his researches provide a useful case study of the antiquarian of the period. His life is a personification of the nexus of social, commercial and intellectual connections previously outlined. His life spanned most of the century and encompassed a wide variety of interests. Apart from acting as Town Clerk of Newcastle for forty-five years, he 'provided the sinews of war for the campaign' of the builder, Richard Grainger to 're-edify'.[3] Newcastle, was active in promoting railway development and held innumerable municipal offices. A potted biography of him entitled 'John Clayton, Lawyer, Antiquary and Man of Letters' is included in Richard Welford's *Men of Mark Twixt Tyne and Tees* and describes 'his stiff and somewhat stately form' dressed invariably in 'a black dress coat, black vest and black trousers, somewhat loose fitting'[4]. His wealth, both inherited and acquired, centred on the family estate at Chesters near Chollerford on the line of Hadrian's Wall, a location which inspired his dedication to Roman antiquities. He joined the Society in 1832, later becoming vice-president, and submitted a series of illustrated reports on his excavations to *Archaeologia Aeliana* which are of major importance in the history of research on the Wall.

Unfortunately, there is little archival material relating to his antiquarian interests. He died without children and succeeding generations, not sharing his passion for things Roman, destroyed family papers and correspondence. An 'autobiography' in the form of a letter to his old school reminiscing on his school life reveals a love of classical learning based on 'solid and excellent grounding in Greek and Latin'.[5] Wallis Budge in his introduction to the Chesters museum guide claims to have drawn on Clayton's papers and quotes his descriptions and remarks verbatim. He portrays a man whose leisure seems as organised as his professional life must have been. 'He devoted the Mondays of each week to the investigation of the remains of the buildings which the Romans had set up'.[6] Many of these remains he subsequently bought and these now constitute most of the principal archaeological sites of the Central Sector of the Wall including the forts of Housesteads, Vindolanda, Carvoran and much of the curtain wall and associated milecastles. The implications of this for the preservation of the remains belong to another chapter. What is important here is his commitment to the furthering of knowledge by the excavation of the sites he acquired and then ensuring the publication of his findings in carefully produced reports for *Archaeologia Aeliana*. Whilst often brief by later standards, they included

FIGURE 1. Portrait of John Clayton from Centenary Edition *Archaeologia Aeliana*, 1913.

maps, plans and accurate drawings of finds and were produced at his own expense. He usually read his own papers at Society meetings. His ideas were therefore open to discussion, although his rather low key and factual approach is often commented upon. Whether the actual excavations were conducted with parallel refinement is doubtful but difficult to establish. There was no agreed methodology at this period. Clayton's main objective was the 'digging out' of stone structures to reveal their plan and make the excavated remains available to visitors. The mode of excavation appears to have been of little concern to Society members and was regarded as being at the discretion of the excavator who might not even be present at most of the proceedings on site. Most of Clayton's excavations were supervised by his foreman, William Tailford, and then later by Tailford's son; Wallis Budge's reference to him as 'this faithful servant' and 'his master's right hand man'[7] reveals much of the relationship between antiquary and digger at this time.

Thus, in John Clayton, we have the private face of nineteenth-century archaeology. A man with the wealth and resources to research for his own pleasure in the context of membership of a society of like-minded men of similar education, geographical origin, professional status and consequently similar attitudes to society. There is limited evidence of any perceived need to convey the fruits of his knowledge outside this confined circle.

By contrast, a study of another notable Society member in the person of the Reverend Doctor John Collingwood Bruce reveals a personality as grandiloquent as his name. In him we have the public, evangelical face of Victorian archaeology. A contemporary and friend of John Clayton, Dr Bruce was the son of the founder of one of Newcastle's most prestigious schools, an institution which he eventually took over despite his training as a medical missionary. The combination of missionary zeal, a background as an educationalist, and training as a preacher in the Presbyterian church came face to face with its life's work in 1848 when, unable to visit France, Dr Bruce took a trip to Hadrian's Wall. The resulting synthesis ultimately produced the most enduring of all popular works on the Wall in the shape of his *Handbook to the Roman Wall* which is still in print and has been updated through numerous editions by a number of distinguished editors. 'He was not a miser, hoarding up his intellectual stores for his own selfish gratification, but a diligent enquirer and a generous distributor of antiquarian lore'.[8] He 'distributed' his interest in the form of public lectures and guided tours, whose great length, alleviated by the odd witticism, was generally appreciated.

Above all, his heart lay with the Newcastle Society which he assiduously attended and addressed, for which he wrote numerous papers and of which he eventually became President. He appears to have had an irrepressible desire to communicate via any media available to him. A number of photographs of him exist and reveal a man of rather Romanesque features and flamboyant appearance, characterised by his plaid worn in a variety of creative modes.

He was not an original thinker in that he drew heavily on the researches of scholars such as John Hodgson who published his *History of Northumberland* in 1840. However, as a publicist, he hit on an original, powerful and enduring concept in the form of the Roman Wall Pilgrimages. The original Pilgrimage took place in 1849, a year after Dr Bruce's initial visit. The circumstances were described by him at a meeting of the Society in 1886. Lectures he had given to the Literary and Philosophical Society, which had many members in common with the Society of Antiquaries, inspired its listeners to wish to visit the Wall and see its wonders for themselves. Winter lectures and summer excursions were a common feature of the period, providing popular education, an opportunity for self improvement and a social outlet for women in particular. Dr Bruce therefore proposed and organised a traverse from end to end of the Wall 'forming a pilgrimage like that described by Chaucer, consisting of both ladies and gentlemen'.[9] His description of the week's excursion indicates a rather festive atmosphere in which eating and drinking figure prominently. Local notables and antiquarians including John Clayton provided hospitality along the way whilst Dr Bruce responded to frequent demands that he should address the attendant 'throng' on the subject of the Wall. Those participating included twenty 'pilgrims proper' including a number invited from outside the area, members of the

FIGURE 2. Portrait of J. Collingwood Bruce from Centenary Edition *Archaeologia Aeliana*, 1913.

FIGURE 3. Portrait of J. Collingwood Bruce. Reproduced by permission of Museum of Antiquities.

Antiquarian Society and most significantly 'many of the gentry resident near the line of our march'. At some important points curiosity drew 'large crowds of the neighbouring population' to observe the proceedings. The attendance of three ladies is specifically recorded. The particular reference to this last fact perhaps indicates an awareness by Dr Bruce of the total absence of any female participation in the normal proceedings of the Society. Such field trips, day excursions and any public lectures seem to have been the sole opportunity available for feminine involvement and women were increasingly taking advantage of it. In subsequent pilgrimages women figure prominently. Another clue to an underlying motivation for promoting such visits comes at the end of Dr Bruce's paper.

In the present day, when the full privileges of citizenship are within the grasp of the humblest members of society, who thus become directly the makers of our country's history, it is well for them to be educated in the past, and to make them mindful of the great memorials which distinguish each era. Our pilgrimage will instruct us and make us the means of instructing others.

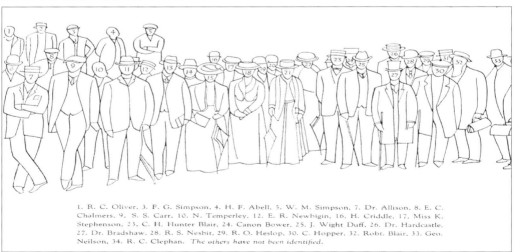

1. R. C. Oliver. 3. F. G. Simpson. 4. H. F. Abell. 5. W. M. Simpson. 7. Dr. Allison. 8. E. C. Chalmers. 9. S. S. Carr. 10. N. Temperley. 12. E. R. Newbigin. 16. H. Criddle. 17. Miss K. Stephenson. 23. C. H. Hunter Blair. 24. Canon Bower. 25. J. Wight Duff. 26. Dr. Hardcastle. 27. Dr. Bradshaw. 28. R. S. Nesbit. 29. R. O. Heslop. 30. C. Hopper. 32. Robt. Blair. 33. Geo. Neilson. 34. R. C. Clephan. *The others have not been identified.*

FIGURE 4. Pilgrims, 1906. Proceedings of the Society of Antiquaries, Newcastle upon Tyne, 4th series, Vol X.

Two connected themes are raised here. The role of Britain's monumental heritage in a newly democratic society and the means by which that society should be educated and informed. In this period, the antiquarian societies were a crucial agency for attempting to fulfil Dr Bruce's aims in that they provided the organisation, coherence and forum for the exchange of ideas and information and the organisational structure to disseminate these ideas via publications, lectures and later the Society's library and museum. This took place, however, within a narrow band of society of which John Clayton was typical but there was also latitude allowed for such as Bruce to take a wider view of which the Pilgrimages were a feature.

The next Pilgrimage of 1886, which established the model for later ones, was, in effect, a tribute to Dr Bruce, then 81, who was made 'Chief Pilgrim' and 'Expounder General'. The visit, a joint operation of the Newcastle and Cumberland and Westmorland Societies, was held in June and started at Wallsend. This was organised on a grander scale than the 1848 event, the group consisting of forty members identified by the wearing of a pilgrim's badge, a silver scallopshell.

FIGURE 5. Pilgrims, 1886. Dr Bruce is seated to the left on a chair. Reproduced by permission of Museum of Antiquities.

Rail travel was now available to certain points from whence carriages
and luggage carts accompanied the pilgrims. A dinner held in the
Great Hall of Newcastle Castle with musical accompaniment inau-
gurated proceedings. Much of the central sector was walked in a
manner rather military. Pilgrims assembled to the sound of a bugle
and were directed, on the western side, by coloured flags where
the line of the vallum and curtain wall was not apparent. Special
excavations in honour of the occasion had been previously carried
out of which the discoveries of John Clayton were most abundant.
The entire event was reported in the papers.

Dr Bruce died in 1892. He had been a dominating figure who had
ensured, by a continuing and unflagging enthusiasm, the health of
archaeology on the Wall. His flair for promotion had ensured a
wider audience and greater sympathy for its research but he had
perhaps outlived his time and usefulness. Eric Birley has seen his
death as a liberating event, referring to the end of his 'pervasive
rule ... His death left the field open for a new generation of antiquaries to try their metal'.[10] He is here speaking as a scholar of the
Wall and is perhaps underestimating the value of the publicity
generated by Dr Bruce who has probably been without parallel as a
promoter of the Wall's cause.

The rise of Eric Birley's 'new generation' is apparent in succeeding
pilgrimages up to World War Two. These occurred at approximately
ten year intervals in 1896, 1906, 1920 and 1930. The excavations visited
in the course of these expeditions were the result of the work of new
names such as Bosanquet, Simpson and Haverfield. These were men
for whom archaeology was a livelihood as well as an interest and
who were developing a self image very different from that of John
Clayton. The days of the antiquary were over.

R. C. Bosanquet who succeeded Clayton as the excavator of
Housesteads, was, as Jim Crow has pointed out, a figure 'spanning
the two worlds from the professional to the gentleman'.[11] He came
from an established, landowning Northumberland family, was
educated at Eton and Trinity and trained as a classical archaeologist
at the British School at Athens, the forcing ground of many British
archaeologists who subsequently practised at home and abroad.
He was placed in charge of the Housesteads excavations by the
Newcastle Society in 1898 and, by 1906, he was Professor of Classical
Archaeology at Liverpool University. His mode of excavation at
Housesteads was not unlike that of John Clayton being geared to
the establishment of the outline structures in order to establish the
internal plan of the fort. This was achieved by 'wall chasing'; stone

FIGURE 6. "Wall Chasing" at Corstopitum, 1908. Reproduced by permission of Corbridge Excavation Fund.

structures were initially located by trenching and then followed by excavating down either side. This was a technique common up to the First World War and was also used at Corbridge, a site which is discussed in Chapter Three.

The transition from enlightened landowner, working on his own initiative in association with an antiquarian society, to a professionally based excavation using scientific methods followed from the First World War and was spearheaded by R. G. Collingwood who, with his combined talents as philosopher, Roman historian and archaeologist, provided for Wall archaeology a sound methodological base. His empirical approach required that research be a problem-solving exercise and that excavation should be designed to answer certain pre-defined questions. As 'interpreter to the learned world',[12] Collingwood was also most effective.

Under Collingwood's guidance, F. G. Simpson became the leading excavator and authority on the Wall. Coming from the manufacturing family of Stead and Simpson, F. G. Simpson trained as an engineer but became dedicated to the study of Hadrian's Wall located close to his work on Tyneside. He served a form of archaeological apprenticeship under J. P. Gibson, a photographer from Hexham and long-standing member of the Newcastle Society. Between them, they developed their own systematic methods of excavation – 'Their work had a new look, as trim as if machined. Trenches were wide, turves and upcast were tidily disposed; the structures revealed were cleared for photography in which Simpson at once set a standard of his own'.[13] Structures and finds were just as carefully recorded. Simpson became Director of Field Studies at the University of Durham and an institutional base for the organisation and financing of excavations came in 1924 with the formation of the Durham University Excavation Committee; directed by Simpson 'the new committee gradually assumed main responsibility for studying the central sector of the Wall, becoming a strong connecting-link between the two Societies and between them and the University of Durham.'.[14] The North of England Excavation Committee was also established in 1924 to ensure the proper recording and supervision of sites and the coordination of excavation in the north. The motivation for this was the need for information for later volumes of the Northumberland County History chaired by Francis Haverfield, Camden Professor of Ancient History at Oxford and Britain's leading Romanist. It is significant that, under Simpson, the supervision of sites was becoming much more professional in this period and a picture of the operation of these committees is provided by their accounts which balance wages against public subscriptions, other takings being minimal.

The increasing influence of university-based scholars such as Collingwood, Simpson and Haverfield who were beginning to give archaeology status as a discipline with its own methods and approaches was parallel to moves in other scientific disciplines such as Geology and Anthropology. Classical History departments such as that at Oxford under Haverfield extended their syllabuses to include archaeology and from these came the next generation of Wall scholars such as I. A. Richmond. In the north, F. G. Simpson founded the School of Romano-British Archaeology at Durham.

The work of these men, backed by the excavation committees, was shown off to the Pilgrimages. By 1930, these could be seen as 'a time for stocktaking and for offering a new programme of research'.[15] Awareness of publicity was also a feature of this Pilgrimage. In the Cumberland and Westmorland Society's report reference is made to 'the growth of public interest in the Wall'.[16] Collingwood produced the book of the Pilgrimage which formed the basis of press reports as well as being an aid to pilgrims. The 1930 Pilgrimage also attracted some distinguished archaeologists including Mortimer Wheeler and Professor Behrens, a noted authority on the German Frontier. Up to 240 people led by Simpson, Bosanquet, and Richmond accompanied by 50 private cars and three motor coaches descended on the Wall resulting in a third-of-a-mile long procession. The fruits of the scientific excavation of the Wall were being exhibited to the world but possibly to an increasingly academic world. An underlying feature of the visit was the threat to quarry on the Wall and the opportunity was there for an exercise in the influencing of public opinion, though its organisers seemed rather reluctant to make it the main issue as this would detract from the scholarly focus of the expedition.

The Centenary Pilgrimage was timed to coincide with the first Congress of Roman Frontier Studies. Numbers had to be restricted to 180. Durham University students were for the first time involved and much was made of the opportunity provided for the cementing of the relationships between the societies and the academics. The Eighth Pilgrimage in 1960 was the inspiration for the publication of the most comprehensive assessment of mural studies to date. Eric Birley's *Research on Hadrian's Wall* remains the standard work of historiography for the Wall and includes an account of the Pilgrimages up to the 1960s.

The Pilgrimages have continued to be held every ten years to the present day and remain a forum for the promotion of the latest research and an opportunity for reassessment and reinterpretation. Whether they continue in the tradition of Bruce and continue to fulfil his original intentions is difficult to assess. The shift in focus of scholarly research from the antiquarian societies to the universities is something he could not have anticipated. Whilst the two antiquarian societies continue to take charge of the organisation of the Pilgrimages, the work they see and the 'expounding' they hear comes from professionals. The repercussions of this shift from antiquarianism to professionalisation are continually reverberating. They had, and have still, enormous implications for the evolution of Hadrian's Wall firstly as an object of research and secondly as a monument with significance well beyond that of playground for privileged antiquarians.

Under the regime of the societies, most excavation had been done at the instigation of individual landowners utilising no agreed methodology and with no final arbiters as to the quality of the work done or of the significance of what was discovered. Most important of all, they had no agreed, coherent framework of research. However, by virtue of their role as social and cultural organisations arising out of their local communities, however restricted they might have been in socio-economic terms, they did recognise a duty to publicise their findings. Interested non-specialists who might be similarly interested in geology, architecture or natural history brought wide-ranging experience to society meetings and excursions and enthusiasts such as Bruce took pleasure in extending peoples' understanding of Hadrian's Wall in particular and archaeology in general. The development of individual, academic disciplines which was such a feature of this period, produced experts who, by initiating the excavation committees, established a control over the direction of Wall archaeology. These scholars, with established bases in their universities rather than the societies, set a rather different agenda from those of the early members of the antiquarian societies. Their monopoly of information and their rising prestige created a potentially powerful pressure group with the capacity to tip the balance in favour of regarding the Wall as primarily an academic resource rather than a place of popular pilgrimage.

A new figure in the equation needs to be introduced when considering the fate of the Wall at this juncture and that is the influence of the State. The government becomes a main player once the issue arises of who actually owns the Wall. This is a question both practical and philosophical as it involves the issue of who *should* own the wall. The following chapter investigates the practical aspects of the issue by looking at a cross-section of excavated sites for which the first question has had markedly different answers.

Notes

1. Philippa Levine, *The Amateur and the Professional*, Cambridge (1986), p. 7.
2. G. Jobey, The Society of Antiquaries of Newcastle on Tyne, *Archaeologia Aeliana* (Fifth series), XVIII (1988), p. 209.
3. 'John Clayton', *Archaeologia Aeliana*, Centenary Volume (1913), p. 183.
4. R. Welford, *Men of Mark Twixt Tyne and Tees*, London (1895), p. 584.

5. Thomas Hodgkin, 'John Collingwood Bruce', *Archaeologia Aeliana* (Second Series), XV (1892), p. 368.

6. E. A. Wallis Budge, *An Account of the Roman Antiquities Preserved in the Museum at Chesters, Northumberland*, London (1907), p. 15.

7. *Ibid.* p. 11.

8. Hodgkin, *Op. cit.*, p. 368.

9. J. C. Bruce, *Proceedings of the Society of Antiquaries*, Vol. 2, No. 25 (1886), p. 136.

10. E. Birley, *Book of the Centenary Pilgrimage of Hadrian's Wall, 4th July – 9th July, 1949*.

11. J. Crow, *Housesteads*, London (1995), p. 109.

12. E. Birley, *Op. cit.*, p. 4.

13. I. A. Richmond, 'F. G. Simpson', *Archaeologia Aeliana* (Fourth Series), XXXIV (1956), p. 220.

14. E. Birley, *Research on Hadrian's Wall*, Kendal (1961), p. 35.

15. *Ibid*, p. 38.

16. *Transactions of the Cumberland and Westmorland Antiquarian and Archaeological Society*, N.S., XXXI, Proceedings, p. 197.

South Gateway, Birdoswald. J. C. Bruce, *The Roman Wall*, 1853.

CHAPTER THREE

Managing an Ancient Monument: Public and Private Enterprise

The problem of the ownership and the associated one of the management of an ancient monument is discussed in this chapter. Peter Fowler has defined the present purpose of monumental management as 'the securing of some sort of future for parts of the surviving past by using a toolkit of statutory, professional and psychological devices, often now supported by the overt interest of an informed and vocal minority in society'.[1] The evolution of this approach is discussed in this and the next chapter by looking at the histories of four prominent Wall sites. Chesters, Housesteads, Corbridge and Vindolanda reveal a complex, varied and often incoherent picture, one subject to endless variables including vested interest, current ideology, money, location and individual will-power. The relationship between the scholarly community, local and national government, and the local population has evolved in a wide variety of ways reflecting the uniqueness of a vast and ever-changing monument.

One of the most venerable sites on the line of the Wall is that of Chesters Roman Station excavated by its owner John Clayton from 1843 and, at intermittent intervals, to the end of his life in 1890. The remains lay in the grounds of his family's estate near Chollerford Bridge, a major crossing point over the River Tyne. His excavations include investigations not only of the fort but of the nearby bath-house and bridge abutment. 'The remains at present visible are in the main a memorial to the Clayton regime'.[2] The site is not well recorded by modern standards although Clayton spasmodically reported his findings to the Newcastle Society and little of it has been dug since. The site also includes the oldest museum on the Wall. Built in 1900, the Clayton Memorial Museum was built to house the finds resulting from Clayton's digs on all his properties including Housesteads. The capacity of his Antiquity House was rapidly overtaken by the results of his enthusiastic excavations which flowed over into his house and garden at some cost to their preservation. The museum, purpose-built in the classical style in the traditions of its time, has remained, more as a result of lassitude on the part of the trustees than by intention, much as it was. Its typological layout of finds is encased in glass cases surrounded by ranks of stone altars, carvings and inscriptions. The pervading air of 'gravitas' makes it a true memorial to Clayton and his antiquarian spirit. Chesters passed into various private ownerships after the entire Clayton estate was dismantled and sold in 1929. The archaeological remains were entrusted to the Ministry of Works in 1954.

A similar, though rather more dynamic and institutionally complex history, applies to Housesteads, also a Clayton property. This is the most widely known of the Wall sites due to the prominence of its situation high on the Whin Sill in the most arrestingly beautiful part of the Wall's central sector. Its past remoteness has facilitated its preservation and it is now the most completely excavated of all the Wall sites. Partly because of its rarity, its ownership, control and management have been a story of Byzantine complexity. The land on which the fort, civilian settlement and museum rest has belonged to the National Trust since 1930; however, the remains themselves are in the guardianship of English Heritage. The whole site is also within the Northumberland National Park.

The farm of Housesteads was bought by John Clayton in 1838 as part of his drive to prevent the further destruction of the surviving remains of the Wall and to further his antiquarian knowlege by their excavation. The results of these diggings are not well recorded. R. C. Bosanquet later excavated on behalf of the Newcastle Antiquaries in a more systematic manner and was followed by the even more meticulous F. G. Simpson. On the auction of the Clayton estate, Housesteads did not achieve a reserve price and was presented to the National Trust. Eric Birley and the Durham University Excavation Committee became involved in research and excavation in the 1930s, a long-standing connection creating an important body of finds which logically had no place at Chesters Museum. The National Trust constructed a new museum adjacent to the fort obscurely designed as a replica of one of the houses excavated in the civilian settlement, though no attempt is made to record this fact on site or use it to any interpretative purpose. Excavations have continued at intervals creating at Housesteads the most extensively exposed and most often visited and high profile site on the Wall. It has been subject to often conflicting pressures and competing interests. Those of the scholars as against those of the visiting public and the requirements of the State are the most prominent and will be discussed in later chapters.

FIGURE 7.
Antiquity House,
Chesters.
Reproduced by
permission of
Museum of
Antiquities.

Corstopitum, a large and unconfined site without the coherence of Housesteads, has been of significance for rather different reasons. It is situated on a main hub of the Roman communications network and had, therefore, both a military and civilian function as the Army's supply base and as a garrison town. The site at Corbridge was first excavated on the initiative of Francis Haverfield whose interest in the preparation of the new County Histories provided the impetus for an investigation of the widespread and complex remains gained with the approval of a local landowner of some influence, J. H. Cuthbert of Beaufront Castle. Commencing in 1906, Haverfield provided the excavation staff from his own undergraduate students thus creating in Corstopitum a training ground for generations of professional archaeologists, including many who went on to play a major part in British archaeology at home and abroad. Oxford's students were taught 'how to conduct excavations, how to handle workmen, and how to deal with and record finds'.[3] The work was financed by the establishment of a special Corbridge Excavation Fund whose trustees worked closely with the Newcastle Society and annual reports were published by Haverfield in *Archaeologia Aeliana*.

These annual summer excavations which persisted until the First World War were documented photographically by J. P. Gibson and

allow an unusual and revealing insight into the social and methodological context of a pre-war, state of the art excavation. Supervisors
included names later to become famous including Leonard Woolley
and Robert Foster, who came from Corbridge and was also a barrister
and novelist. The hard work was done by untrained, local labourers
numbering between six and twenty-five men who were supervised
by the students and worked for wages. Clothing demonstrates the
sharp social distinctions involved. The tools of the trade, shovels,
pickaxes, crowbars and brooms rather than trowels removed the
spoil which was transported by wheelbarrow and rail carts.

Haverfield was the first to see the need for the practical training
of future archaeologists in Britain and the tradition was carried on
by F. G. Simpson. In 1934 investigations restarted but in the context
of state custody under the Ancient Monuments Department which
had acquired the site by deed of gift from Mr Cuthbert who gave
up all but the hunting rights. The Department was required to
'disengage for consolidation' the remains in the course of which
the Chief Inspector of Ancient Monuments, J. P. Bushe-Fox who
had himself trained at Corstopitum, invited Durham University
to continue excavations under
the direction of F. G Simpson.
Simpson saw the potential of
Haverfield's annual summer
training courses as a means
of carrying out a long-term,
planned programme of re-
search whilst still training
archaeologists. The site now
also had the advantage that
there was no limit to access
or to time, the only limit being
the inaccessibility of the previously consolidated areas.
Archaeological activity continued every season except
during World War Two on
into the 1970s and continued
to involve Britain's most
eminent Romanists including
Eric Birley, Ian Richmond and
later J. P. Gillam of Newcastle
University.

FIGURE 8.
Chesters
Museum, 1902.
E. A. Wallis
Budge *An
Account of the
Roman
Antiquities
preserved in the
Museum at
Chesters
Northumberland*,
London, 1907.

The site of Corstopitum is infinitely complex and has produced, over the years, a large body of information and a large collection of finds. The finds have caused considerable problems. They were first housed in a timber and corrugated iron building in 1913. This was refurbished by Eric Birley in the 1930s with money from the Office of Works. The intention to supply something more permanent had then been under discussion but it took fifty years before a new museum was built in 1983 by the Trustees and the Department of the Environment, an example of one of the few large-scale capital investments in building by the State on the Wall.

On the whole these three sites represent the official face of monument management. They have similar patterns of transition from the private ownership of gentlemen archaeologists into public ownership by the Second World War. The succeeding policy has generally been one of preservation and care tending to the stereotypical image of manicured lawns, neat signs, uniformed attendants and limited amenities. Digging has been carefully organised by the universities for their own purposes and in cooperation with state institutions. This picture tends to the scholarly rather than the popular end of the spectrum.

FIGURE 9.
Chesters Museum, 1995. Photograph by Alison Ewin.

A contrasting picture is obtained from a study of a site which, rather than being located in a remote, rural setting, is urban and consequently subject to very different pressures. At South Shields, there was a need from the start for popular support and interest to be finely balanced with the needs of scholarly investigation. South Shields is the site of a fort, built to protect the entrance to the Tyne and serve as port and supply base for the eastern end of the wall zone. By the middle of the nineteenth century, the area had become part of industrial Tyneside and was thoroughly urbanised. The process of excavation and development here was very much at

variance with the previously described practice of wealthy antiquarians such as John Clayton. The Newcastle Society was however on
the doorstep and played an important part as events unfolded.

The initiator of the serious research of this site was a man of
rather different stamp from John Clayton and Collingwood Bruce.
Robert Blair was born in South Shields in 1845 and was the son of
a river pilot. He was in many ways a self-made man, training as a
solicitor at the Mechanics Institute of South Shields. He joined
the Newcastle Society at twenty-nine becoming its secretary and
then editor of its publications, a post he held for forty years. His
involvement in the South Shields excavations came at the start of
his career and he kept a diary of the proceedings which included
numerous sketches of the finds. He appears to have been a man of
great enthusiasm with a gift for publicity and was a friend and
correspondent of Dr Bruce.

In 1875 land containing the fort site, known locally as the Lawe
and belonging to the Ecclesiastical Commissioners, was made available for building. As building commenced, treasure-hunting river
pilots quickly unearthed a complete Roman column. Dr Hoopell, a
fellow antiquary combined with Blair to publicise the possibilities
of this site for excavation reporting in a letter to the *Shields Gazette*
of 20 February, 1875, that a Samian bowl had been found on the site
of a house then being erected. 'This is in the possession of Mr Brown,
grocer … and may be seen by the curious in the window of his
shop'.[4] A public meeting was held and chaired by the Mayor of South
Shields. An exploration committee was set up with Blair as Secretary
and a subscription list started which included Bruce and Clayton. It
was agreed that all finds should go to the Free Library of South
Shields. The excavations, using labour provided by the building
contractors, were extensively reported in the local papers and seem
to have become a source of great interest to the local population,
'Yesterday the camp was visited by many thousands of persons'[5]
so much so that a policeman was needed to guard the site. Dr Bruce
visited the excavations and generally joined in with his usual enthusiasm. The new Library of Natural History and Antiquities was
opened in 1876 to house the finds. Blair reports that Roman remains
jostled for attention with boomerangs, assagys, and a model of the
lifeboat.

The site was neither back-filled nor built on and, in 1878, Dr
Hoopell wrote of its neglect referring to stone robbing and vandalism
by children. The case for its preservation was eloquently expressed
by Hoopell and, in many ways, echoes Bruce.

the only thing remembered will be that the thriving, populous and ought-to-be cultured town of South Shields had within its borders a citadel of Roman power, a relic and witness of its own greatness and importance in far-off days, a powerful attraction to visitors and priceless educational boon for its own children and through apathy or devotion to all-absorbing monetary pursuits, suffered it to be wiped out, to be swept away, to be stamped out of its midst.[6]

The Town Council was finally persuaded in 1880 to turn the site into a 'People's Roman Remains Park', a concept which expanded with the building of a special museum on the site in 1953. This was opened with some éclat by Sir Mortimer Wheeler the event being televised and widely reported. Wheeler was then President of the South Shields Archaeological and Historical Society. This provided a base for a South Shields Archaeological and Historical Society which still flourishes today. Newcastle University students in conjunction with the Archaeological Society under John Gillam excavated parts of the civilian settlement in 1970. Further areas of the fort were excavated on the demolition of adjacent streets and the Park was thus extended.

Ian Richmond wrote a guide to the site and in 1975 the Park was taken over by the Tyne and Wear Museums Service. In this way the traditional support of local government was continued but with the independence to extend its services. This included a proposal to reconstruct the West Gate of the fort. This would be the first reconstruction of a standing remain associated with Hadrian's Wall and was consequently controversial. Professional archaeologists such as Charles Daniels claimed that it would compromise future excavations and was anyway unlikely to be accurate. Official objections from the Historic Buildings Commission on the grounds that the proposals would be 'a major departure from accepted procedure for looking after ancient monuments' – that is, that all remains should be 'conserved as found'[7] – forced a public enquiry in 1984. Reassurances were made that the underlying remains would be protected by concrete foundations and a West German archaeologist testified to the success of the Saalburg museum which includes an extensive on-site reconstruction of a fortress on the German sector of the Roman frontier system. The plan of the gate was known in detail and the reconstruction design was based on the extant gates of two forts on the African frontier in Libya. Correct building materials were used in the form of local sandstone and freshly cut oak for the external timberwork. The Department of the Environment allowed the project to go ahead as an experiment which should be carefully monitored. The gate was constructed by John Laing and opened in 1988 with some ceremonial, having cost around £500,000.

South Shields' Roman remains are a story of civic pride which has regarded the excavations as a local responsibility which was on the whole cherished, if occasionally neglected. In effect, the town has ensured the survival of the remains for over a century providing an amenity of educational value and a community focus. Attempts have been consistently made to be genuinely popular and relevant to the local population as a whole, maintaining the vision of Blair and Hoopell. At times this has been at variance with some academic opinion; however, there is not necessarily a monolithic scholarly viewpoint in existence, as may be demonstrated by the study of a further site.

The site of Chesterholm, now referred to by its Roman name of Vindolanda, is a pre-Hadrianic fort lying to the south of the Wall on the original line of the Stanegate. It was one of the earliest remains subject to antiquarian research starting in 1818 with Anthony Hedley described by Eric Birley as 'the pioneer in the methodical investigation of the internal layout of Roman forts'.[8] A clergyman and

FIGURE 10. Excavations at South Shields, 1875. The Excavation Committee. Reproduced by permission of Museum of Antiquities.

member of the Newcastle Antiquarian Society, Hedley built a cottage next to the site which became a Mecca for mural researchers. The Clayton Estate added Chesterholm to its stable of monuments on the death of Hedley and, on the estate's dispersal in 1929, it was bought by a young Eric Birley who excavated it and published the results in *Archaeologia Aeliana*. The removal of the Birley family resulted in the site being placed in State guardianship, consolidated and scheduled as an ancient monument in 1939. The rest of the Chesterholm land was farmed and therefore inaccessible to the public and the remains seemed destined to slumber undisturbed in their hidden valley away from the hubbub of nearby Housesteads.

The site sprang to prominence only when Eric Birley's son, Robin, followed up information provided by J. K. St. Joseph's aerial photographs of 1949 which indicated extensive building to the west of the fort. Long negotiations enabled short-term excavations in the late 1960s; however, the situation was revolutionised when a sympathetic parent of one of the diggers, Mrs Daphne Archibald, bought the estate from the farmer and gave the land under excavation to a newly formed trust for the purposes of further excavation. The Vindolanda Trust directed by Robin Birley 'started with a small wooden hut,

FIGURE 11. Excavations at South Shields, 1875. Reproduced by permission of Museum of Antiquities.

FIGURE 12. Sir
Mortimer Wheeler
before his
Presidential
Address to the
South Shields
Archaeological and
Historical Society,
1956. Reproduced
by permission of
Shields Gazette.

which doubled as tool-shed and shelter for the excavators, and a
mixed assortment of spades, picks, shovels and wheelbarrows and
nothing in the Bank'.[9] What had been a seasonal project became
full-time work financed solely by revenue from visitor admissions
and the Friends of Vindolanda who received regular information on
and tours of the site.

Robin Birley's approach to the excavation of Vindolanda was a
revolutionary one for which there are no other parallels on the Wall.
Its history has proved often controversial and has involved the
fostering of a culture at variance with that of the establishment
sites of Housesteads and Chesters. Its market-driven approach has
entailed a careful consideration of the requirements of its visitors
and the story of the excavation of the civilian settlement has received
wide and coordinated publicity reminiscent of Hoopell and Blair in
South Shields, though a wider range of media has been available.
Visits from 'Blue Peter', reports on television news as well as in
national and local papers all contributed to Vindolanda's increasing
fame through the 1970s.

Within the context of raising money, the Trust's declared aims
include the excavation, preservation and display of remains and finds
on site, the education of the public in Roman archaeology and history
and the training of students of archaeology. A concern for education
was a feature from the start. In conjunction with Gateshead Education Authority, the Trust initiated a programme using school

children to excavate and to help build a reconstruction turf wall. Later the Manpower Services Commission also provided workers. Even less conventional was the use of a JCB to remove the layers of clay and rubble used by Roman engineers to seal the site of the previous fort before rebuilding. This sealing process was proving to be of great archaeological significance in that it created anaerobic conditions in which vast quantities of organic material were preserved including the famous writing tablets, the interpretation of which revolutionised the documentary record of the Wall.

For some scholars this was not the acceptable face of Roman archaeology. A frontal assault was launched by Grace Simpson, daughter of F. G. Simpson, in 1974. A letter appeared in *The Times*[10]

FIGURE 13. The opening of the reconstruction of the West Gate of South Shields Fort 1988. Collection of South Shields Public Library.

which referred to the use of a JCB to 'tear huge holes in the stratified Roman deposits'. It described the excavations as 'treasure hunting', the site as an 'open cast quarry' and spoke of an atmosphere of 'over excitement and excess of publicity'. She criticised the use of school children as excavators and described the replicas as 'monstrosities'. The underlying implication was that important sites should not be entrusted to private enterprise. The case of Vindolanda became something of a *cause célèbre* amongst the Wall cognoscenti and crystallised the debate over private versus public ownership of wall monuments. Meeting the expectations of visitors, who were sorely needed for their money, was seen as conflicting with the rigours of scholarly research. The debate proceeded in *The Times* and elsewhere resulting in a libel action being brought by three of the Trustees, including Professor Barri Jones, against the editor of *The Times*. This was upheld and, after an inspection by members of the Ancient Monuments Board, Robin Birley's approach to Vindolanda was to some degree vindicated.

Vindolanda has remained a site in which excavation has been a continuing feature. The publicity given to its finds and the opportunity to see digging in progress created visitor numbers on a par with Housesteads. The site now has its own museum and research facilities, interestingly enough located in the house of Chesterholm which had been Robin Birley's childhood home. The Vindolanda Trust also runs the nearby site of Cavoran, a fort on the line of the Wall, which remains unexcavated but has a farmhouse close by now converted to house the Roman Army Museum which has become a popular attraction for tourists and school parties.

Thus the pattern of development is an inconsistent one. The rise of professional archaeology, whilst refining a coherent methodology and providing some consensus on a framework for research, has not brought with it a coherent approach to the relationship between the needs of research, the fate of the sites where this research takes place and the obligation recognised by Bruce and Blair via the antiquarian societies to communicate with a wider public than the narrow stratum of academia attending Frontier Conferences and the later Pilgrimages.

The vagaries of ownership combined with the machinations of individuals have produced a spectrum of monument management from State control to local government control to private enterprise, from Chesters to South Shields to Vindolanda with many other sites not mentioned in this work having their own place within it. State control has enabled the academic community to advance its aims as at Corstopitum; however, it is questionable whether such control has always met the needs of the visiting public, as the popularity of Vindolanda has demonstrated.

Notes

1. P. Fowler, *The Past in Contemporary Society*, London (1992), p. 10.
2. E. Birley, *Chesters Roman Fort Official Guide-book*, London (1960), p. 4.
3. F. Haverfield, *Proceedings of the Society of Antiquaries of London*, Vol. 2 XXIII, p. 478.
4. *Shields Gazette*, 20 February 1875.
5. *Shields Gazette*, 22 March 1875.
6. R. E. Hoopell, 'On the Discovery and Exploration of the Roman Remains at South Shields in the Year 1875–6,' *Transactions of the Natural History Society of Northumberland, Durham and Newcastle*, Vol. VIII (1878), p. 126–167.
7. *Newcastle Journal*, 30 November 1984.
8. E. Birley, *Research on Hadrian's Wall*, Kendal (1961), p. 185.
9. R. Birley, *The Making of Modern Vindolanda with the Life and Work of Anthony Hedley 1777–1835*, Greenhead (1995), p. 67.
10. *The Times*, 23 April 1974.

Milestone at Chesterholm. J. C. Bruce, *The Roman Wall*, 1853.

CHAPTER FOUR

Defining an Ancient Monument: Preservation to Reconstruction

A major issue affecting changes in ownership and hence the evolution of the various sites has been the problem of what to do with them once excavated. Whilst individuals and institutions have sought to observe, research and excavate the Wall, its conservation is a separate issue with implications both institutional and ideological. One of the themes running through the case histories outlined in Chapter Three is the correlation between state interference and the increasingly perceived need for the preservation of archaeological sites. The 'vocal minority' referred to by Peter Fowler has been instrumental in the move to state control. Even the National Trust was not considered a suitable institution to be entrusted with a Roman remain. In a letter to *The Times* written after his attendance at the 1949 Pilgrimage, R. E. Mortimer Wheeler wrote to complain of 'the shabby, uncared-for aspect of the famous Roman fort at Housesteads' which he considered, strongly contrasted with the aspect of Ministry of Works sites such as Chollerford Bridge Abutment at Chesters. He also referred to the 'deplorably ruinous condition' of 'other well known structures still in private hands'.[1] The terminology associated with conservation is varied with remarkably subtle and complex undertones. Remains may be 'preserved', 'consolidated', 'reconstructed' and 'replicated'. The word 'conservation' itself has become a term charged with powerful emotional and ideological connotations.

Fundamentally, 'preservation' is linked to the inevitable decay of any structure. The need to prevent further dereliction may arise from the effect of erosion, both man-made and natural, or from the effect of wilful destruction which may arise from economic, political or cultural circumstances. When discussing archaeological sites a further dimension must be considered. The process of archaeological excavation, by exposing what was previously hidden, is instantly destructive and preservation is not possible without some consolidation, a process often indistinguishable from reconstruction.

John Clayton's excavations of the curtain wall, for instance, have left a legacy of 'Clayton Wall' which is neither Hadrianic nor Severan. In an ironic way, archaeology, in the process of investigating the past, creates something new as a byproduct of its actions; a relic not previously there. It is at this point that the interests of the scholar and the public are likely to diverge. Once recorded, an excavated site loses its meaning as an object of research and becomes something else, a 'monument'. The means by which an ancient monument is created requires an understanding of the ways in which remains come to be conserved and the context in which people and institutions make their decisions. The following account of the conservation of the Wall will hopefully illustrate this process.

The psychological roots of the need society has to retain the relics of its past are difficult to define but have recently been interestingly explored by commentators such as David Lowenthal. 'A past lacking tangible relics seems too tenuous to be credible'.[2] Monuments have a reassuring quality in that they demonstrate that there was a past and that it was different from the present. The idea of relics as witnesses to past events and with a concreteness that gives immediacy in three dimensions is something not achievable in a history book. They also 'enlarge landscapes'[3] by juxtaposing past and present. These landscapes may be the rural, rugged ones of Housesteads Fort or the urban, industrialised one of South Shields; the experience is different but of equal significance.

Thus remains need to be preserved as monuments for reasons other than their intrinsic archaeological significance. Conceptually, a monument is an almost indefineable but neverthless powerful entity, an icon representing a society's vision of its past. Statutorily, a monument is what the government says it is; if it is on a scheduled list then it is a 'monument' and merits the protection of the state. How it becomes scheduled, protected, then preserved is often a matter of chance but a key feature is any perceived threat to its existence which can mobilise the forces of public opinion, though not necessarily academic opinion. An additional theme is the growing distrust of private enterprise as an appropriate guardian for important monuments. This has already been partly illustrated by the histories of, for example, Chesters and Housesteads. However, it perhaps deserves closer analysis.

A survey of the changing state of the Wall's remains since the eighteenth century, as with its topography, is one of ups and downs. Whilst the State is currently avowedly dedicated to the Wall's preservation, it has also been responsible for probably the greatest single act of destruction in its two thousand year history. An act enabling the building of 'a Road Proper for the Passage of Troops and Carriages' from Carlisle to Newcastle was passed following a survey of current roads in 1749. The inability of government troops to intercept Prince Charles' march south in 1745 combined with a petition from the local gentry on the grounds that the roads between the two towns were 'uncultivated, thinly inhabited and impassable'.[4] The fact that the line chosen sought to avoid damage to surrounding agricultural land reflects the priorities and vested interests of the period. Dismantling the stone work of the wall, using the remains as the foundation of the new road and reusing the Roman stone for its surfacing ensured that the construction costs were low and the road straight, at least for the first 30 miles out of Newcastle until the Whin Sill was reached by the Wall.

Such destruction did not go unremarked. William Stukeley, an early antiquarian, was also an early conservationist. He toured the Wall in 1725 and in his diaries[5] he refers to a conversation with the Princess of Wales at Carlton House expressing concern at 'the havoc now making of this noble antiquity'. The surveyors 'pull the cut and squared stones of the wall down and beat 'em to pieces with sledge hammers'. Unfortunately his efforts thus to create a public opinion starting at the top had no effect. His later account of his tour outlines his attitude to the purposes of preservation which were to

> revive the Roman glory amongst us, and may serve to invite noble minds to endeavour to that merit and public spiritedness which shine through all their actions. This tribute at least we owe them, and they deserve it at our hands, to preserve their remains.[6]

Throughout the eighteenth and into the nineteenth century a more gradual process of attrition affected the Wall. Agricultural improvements required quantities of stone for building field walls and farm buildings. William Hutton, a Birmingham historian and traveller, walked the Wall in 1802 claiming to be the first to do so. Near Halton Chesters, approaching the central sector of the Wall, he came upon the destruction of a section seven and a half feet high by a local landowner, Henry Tulip Esq., who needed the stone to build a farmhouse. Hutton reports a request for him to desist from 'putting an end to the most noble monument of Antiquity in the whole Island'.[7] In the conclusion to his account he states 'The ruins have suffered more during the last century, than in the fifteen before.'[8] The story of Henry Tulip's attack on the Wall has a happy ending as Dr John Lingard in his unpublished notes of a visit in 1800 remarks that thirty-five yards of wall remained in H. Tulip's grounds.[9]

The present state of preservation on the central sector of the Wall probably owes most to John Clayton. Much of its survival resulted from his early walks along the wall which revealed the extent of the quarrying. Landowners had no incentive to take steps to prevent robbing by their tenants, and unfortunately it was usually the facing stones at waist height and most conveniently transported that were robbed leaving the core to decay. John Clayton's decision to arrest the destruction by buying up any land associated with the Wall must be the single greatest act of conservation in the history of the Wall or, for that matter, of archaeology in Britain. It was an action with few precedents and arose from a commitment the origins of which are difficult to determine. Clayton seems to have been a very private man and has left no account of his life. His action was not typical of the estate owners of his time and there is no real evidence of any tide of pro-conservation public opinion. Maybe antiquarian curiosity combined with immediately available wealth enabled a self-indulgence of which conservation was merely a by-product.

The evidence of public opinion really evolving comes with the Pilgrimage of 1930. Eric Birley refers to the strenuous efforts made by both societies to prevent the destruction liable to happen with the floating of the quarrying company of 'Roman Stone Limited', an ill-omened name. Extensive destruction of the Wall had already occurred where the whinstone outcrops at Cawfields and Walltown in the central sector and the extension of Britain's road system created a demand for road-stone which made further quarrying commercially attractive. The issue was raised in *The Times* of July 1930 in a letter inviting the minister concerned, Mr Lansbury, to protect the Wall from the feared predations on 'that great national monument'. It was signed by, among others, Rudyard Kipling, John Buchan, and Josiah Wedgewood. Following questions in the House, a bill to protect the surroundings of ancient monuments was passed with the appointment of commissioners of works providing protection pending legislation. This strengthening of the Ancient Monuments Act limited the area in which quarrying was allowed but did not ban it from the whole area. The case for local employment in an area recently deprived of its coal mining industry was a strong incentive to allow it at the time. What is significant is the creating of a climate of opinion by an influential sector of society unconnected with archaeology, though aided by the publicity given to the 1930 Pilgrimage, forcing the government to recognise the significance of Hadrian's Wall as a monument so important as to merit its own legislation. In 1943 a government order was needed to stop quarrying at Walltown Crags and the Vallum and Wall were protected along a mile-wide strip. In 1991 a public enquiry into an application by Arco Britain to drill a bore hole near Corbridge was refused by the Environment Secretary. The reclamation of the quarried site at Cawfields was initiated by the National Park in 1972.

We see here a drive to preservation, which was initiated by antiquarian research gradually coming to be seen as the responsibility of the state in the twentieth century mainly due to the force of public opinion. A look at the legislation reveals the reluctance of government to take this on. The 1882 Ancient Monuments Protection Act was voluntary and did not affect the absolute rights of the property owners. It was drawn up by General Pitt Rivers and

FIGURE 14. Advertisement in *Jenkinson's Practical Guide to Carlisle, Gilsland, Roman Wall and Neighbourhood*, London, 1875.

listed mainly prehistoric remains. The 1913 Act had more bite with the setting up of advisory boards and an inspectorate. In the case of the Roman Wall, much government intervention has been reactive rather than proactive. The significance of Hadrian's Wall was not, in fact, recognised until quite late. It was not listed until a short section was scheduled in the Fifth List of Ancient Monuments of 1925 but effective legal protection was really granted only with the 'Roman Wall and Vallum Preservation Order' of 1931 in response to the threat of quarrying. Most of the major sites such as Chesters, Corbridge and Housesteads have come under state or National Trust control 'by deed of gift' from landowners wishing to off-load the responsibility of the inherited fruits of a previous generation's antiquarian obsessions, whilst keeping the shooting rights, of course.

Having reluctantly taken the care of this ancient monument onboard, the state, or the managers appointed by the state, have to decide whether they are willing to take the plunge or just dip their toe in the waters of public accountability. This accountability is in many ways a dual one. Firstly there is a commitment to conserve the remains for the benefit of present and future generations, an issue already discussed. Secondly, once conserved, the sites will be visited and will require explanation. The debate over how this should be done continues to be controversial and relates to the previously raised question of who the Wall is for. If it is ostensibly in public ownership, it should be managed in the interests of the public; however, what constitutes the public is hard to define and the success of Vindolanda might indicate that private enterprise is more in line with the public's present needs. An analysis of the means by which the Wall has been explained to the public from the antiquarians to the present day follows in the next chapter.

Notes

1. *The Times*, 15 July 1949.
2. D. Lowenthal, *The Past is a Foreign Country*, Cambridge (1985), p. 247.
3. *Ibid*, p. 248 .
4. Quoted W. Lawson, 'The Construction of the Military Road in Northumberland 1745–1757', *Archaeologia Aeliana* (Fifth Series), II (1973).
5. W. Stukeley, Diaries, Vol. 3 (Surtees Society).
6. W. Stukeley, Iter Boreale, quoted S. Piggott, *William Stukeley*, Oxford (1950) p. 76.

7. William Hutton, *The History of the Roman Wall*, London (1813), re-printed 1990, p. 56.
8. *Ibid*, p. 78.
9. R. C. Bosanquet, 'J. Lingard, Notes Transcribed and Annotated', *Archaeologia Aeliana* (Fourth Series) VI (1929).

Housesteads (Borcovicus) from the east. J. C. Bruce, *The Roman Wall*, 1853.

CHAPTER FIVE

Explaining an Ancient Monument: Interpretation

'Relics render the past more important but not better known'
D. Lowenthal, *The Past is a Foreign Country* [1]

Once the institutions have been evolved for the excavation, conservation and administration of Wall sites, as monuments they need to be prepared for consumption. The vital function of mediating between the scholar and the knowledge gained from archaeological research and those wishing to see and understand the physical remains it leaves behind is currently termed 'interpretation'. This is a term much in vogue but is a concept as old as the discoveries themselves. Ruins in many ways do not speak for themselves, they remain mute in the face of popular ignorance both of the significance of the remains themselves and of the process by which they came into being. That it is the responsibility of the historian to explain such things was current under Dr Bruce but is one perhaps lost during the period of professionalisation up to the post war period. Interpretation was expressed in the terminology of the academic establishment rather than the likely visitor. However, if previously many sites were seen as belonging intellectually to the archaeologists this is certainly no longer the case. For social, cultural and ideological reasons, the duty towards the visitor is increasingly paramount. The accepted response to the question 'Who is the Wall for?' has changed. This chapter seeks to outline the changing approaches taken by both scholars and non specialists to interpretation. The media available and technology have changed though the format has in some ways remained remarkably the same.

The most long-standing instrument has been the guide book and here Dr Bruce's influence is still pervasive. A byproduct of the Pilgrimages was the associated *Hand-Book to the Roman Wall*, itself a byproduct of his magisterial work *The Roman Wall*. The original in the first edition of 1863 was termed the *Wallet Book*, its purpose being to assist pilgrims to trace the monument's remains. Its format consisted of an introduction looking at the historical sources, an overview of different categories of structure such as the 'vallum', 'murus' and 'station' followed by a 'local description' of each section along the line of the Wall going from east to west and designed for those investigating on foot. The whole was illustrated with engravings depicting the remains, the associated finds, plus plans and maps. The handbook is still in print today and, in R. G. Collingwood, I. A. Richmond and Charles Daniels, there is a line of editors representing three generations of the foremost Wall authorities which must testify to its continuing prestige. Collingwood points out that successive updatings have diluted the vigorous prose of the original in which 'the descriptions are vivid and terse; the style is rapid and eloquent'.[2] The immediacy and the anecdotal quality of the work has necessarily been lost as research is updated and integrated into the site descriptions. The illustrations were woodcuts and copper engravings, though the latter went out of use after the first few editions having worn away, and in 1895 the first photographs were introduced.

The use of illustration was a vital aspect of the work of the antiquarians, not just as a means of interpretation, but as a vital method of recording in detail finds and structures in the absence of photographs of any quality. Subsequently these illustrations have been of importance as a record of a period in which much has disappeared. Museums were in their infancy; altars and inscriptions were kept in back gardens and finds in private collections later dispersed. The archaeological society journals are lavishly illustrated with photography only gradually supplementing and replacing line illustrations. Early reproductions of photographs in the handbook are less than successful.

More detailed and focussed guides came with the advent of Ministry control of certain sites. These uniform publications held sway pretty well unchallenged until the 1960s. They had all the allure of a civil service manual. The official guide to Corbridge was first published in 1935. The text was written by Eric Birley, it ran to 26 pages and consisted of a chronological history of the site followed by what was essentially a

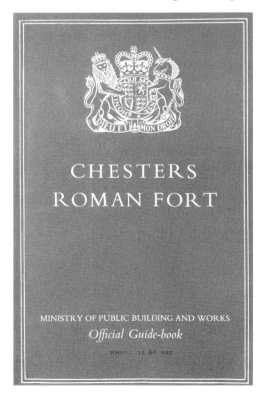

FIGURE 15. Official Guide-book, Chesters Roman Fort, 1960. Reproduced by permission of English Heritage.

CHESTERS ROMAN FORT

MINISTRY OF PUBLIC BUILDING AND WORKS
Official Guide-book
HMSO : 1s. 6d. NET

FIGURE 16.
"Irregular Scouts
and Raetian
auxiliaries, 3rd
Century".
R. Embleton, artist.
Reproduced by
permission of Frank
Graham.

description of the standing remains. The text was written rather like an academic treatise using the language of the architect and engineer with a scattering of 'chamfered plinths', 'abutments' and 'pediments'. There were 27 dates and four photographic illustrations, one of the West Granary, three of finds, and a plan after Knowles one of the pre-war excavators, with no key and an unreadable scale. By 1954 the site plan had been enlarged with a key and four different photographs; otherwise it was much the same. The 1977 edition was on shiny paper, was still by Eric Birley but with more and better photographs. The guide was finally rewritten for English Heritage by J. N. Dore in 1989. The format was changed to that of a written 'conducted tour' of the site. It has only eight dates, slightly less

FIGURE 17. "Reconstruction of Latrines – Housesteads Fort". R. Embleton, artist. Reproduced by permission of Frank Graham.

complex language, 29 illustrations including eight aerial photographs and eight pages on the museum structured thematically along the lines of 'life in Roman Corbridge'.

All HMSO guides to Wall sites were written by Eric Birley to identical formats. They appear to envisage a readership both highly literate, committed and already historically knowledgeable. They contrast quite considerably with the publications of the private sector, most notably those written by Robin Birley for Vindolanda and by Les Turnbull, a teacher who was in charge of the Gateshead project to involve schoolchildren in excavation at Vindolanda. These guides have a strong sense of their audience, are written as a straightforward narrative and explain the processes and purpose of excavation from the point of view of someone deeply involved in the process and writing with an educational motive. The language is different but the atmosphere created is closer to that of Bruce than Eric Birley.

A coherence of approach to these unofficial publications was achieved by the publisher, Frank Graham, also a one-time teacher, who set up his firm locally in Jesmond in the 1970s. His interest in

FIGURE 18. "Milecastle 42, Cawfields, 1848" by R. B. Richardson. J. C. Bruce *The Roman Wall*, 1853.

FIGURE 19. "Pons Aelii, Restored" by H. B. Richardson, Lithograph by J. Storey. J. C. Bruce *The Roman Wall*, 1853.

FIGURE 20.
"Building the
Wall".
R. Embleton,
artist.
Reproduced by
permission of
Frank Graham.

all things Roman is apparent in his catalogue of guides and books. What also made them distinctive and immediately appealing was his use of the illustrations of R. Embleton who produced vivid, dynamic reconstructions of the people of the Frontier. He was careful to paint using existing archaeological evidence. The large and diverse organic finds at Vindolanda had made this exercise more meaningful particularly when it came to depicting every day civilian and military dress. Embleton produced books, posters, and postcards in their millions and they still sell today. His portrayal of the occupants of the latrines at Housesteads is still beloved of all schoolchildren.

This emphasis on visual impact was also a feature of Bruce's

FIGURES 21 & 22. "Bath House, Cilurnum" and "Castle Nick, Milecastle". Postcards produced by Gibson & Son. Reproduced by permission of Northumberland Record Office.

attitude to interpretation. His original pilgrimage of 1849 had been in the company of two local artists, H. B. and T. M. Richardson whose watercolours of the Wall Bruce used to illustrate his lectures delivered the following winter. They were used in the same way as slides are today. They were also used to illustrate his magnum opus *The Roman Wall*, a number being converted into engravings by the lithographer, John Storey. On the whole they represented the remains 'as seen' although an educational dimension was added with reconstructed scenes, a tradition carried on by Alan Sorrell in the twentieth century and also R. Embleton.

The impact of photography on interpretation was, of course, immense and Bruce, and popularisers ever since, have used 'lantern slides' as a major aspect of any lecture. The ability to project an image to the size required by the venue facilitated any exposition greatly. A further application of photography to popularisation was the introduction of the postal system and consequently of the ubiquitous postcard. Fortunately, in the Gibson family, the Wall found skilled and knowledgeable photographers who recorded it with both accuracy and artistry. J. P. Gibson was a Hexham chemist who became an authority on the Wall and its excavation. He was Vice President of the Newcastle Society of Antiquaries and a frequent contributor to *Archaeologia Aeliana*. His interest in photography started early in life in 1860 and he became a distinguished exponent of both landscape and architectural subjects probably on a par with his contemporary, Frank Meadow Sutcliff, in Whitby.

The two interests of archaeology and photography came together towards the end of the century when Gibson began to record every aspect of the exploration of the Wall. His landscapes, views of the remains which he had excavated as well as those of his fellow antiquaries, and photographs of finds later added to by his son John, form a vast archive consisting of negatives, prints, lantern slides, and postcards.

The complexity of the early technology makes these pictures a remarkable achievement and they represent a unique record of mural studies at the turn of the century. His photographs were used extensively in later editions of Bruce's Handbook and the use of photography to circulate images in guides, publicity material and in museum displays has of course increased with the ease of production, the use of colour and the cheapness of printing.

Though not precisely a medium, an influential phenomenon which has greatly aided the interpretation and understanding of the Wall and its structures has been the contribution made by those who have surveyed and mapped the region. George Mark surveyed and prepared maps for Horsley's *Britannia Romana* of 1732. The building of the military road in the 1750s prompted another survey. In 1853 Henry MacLauchlan surveyed the whole wall on the orders of the Duke of Northumberland. This is visually the most stunning of the Wall maps and formed the basis of the maps used in the Handbook. The Ordnance Survey's contribution has been enormous in that by habitually marking archaeological sites on its popular maps it has raised awareness of the past as well as aiding those wishing to locate specifically known features. In 1964 the Ordnance Survey produced its only map of a single monument, 'marvellously depicted in its frontier context in a wide swathe across northern England'.[3] This has been recently updated and, though no longer the model of clarity of the original, it is a vital tool for both the archaeologist and the visitor.

The most prestigious, expensive and often controversial feature of interpetation has been, from the beginning, the setting up and maintenance of museums. From its foundation, the Society of Antiquaries of Newcastle made the ownership of its own museum a priority; however, it was not until 1834 that the Society found a

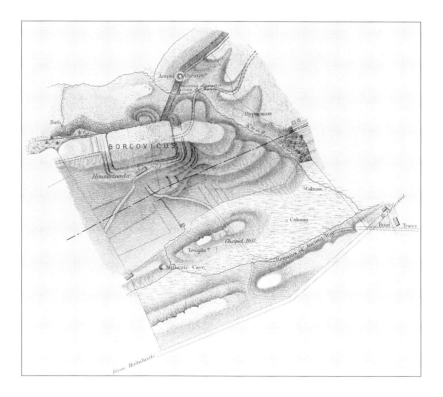

FIGURE 23. MacLaughlan's survey of Housesteads – 1852/1854. Revised in J. C. Bruce *The Roman Wall*, 1867.

location in the Keep of the Castle. 'Our Roman treasures hitherto
ranged round the grass-plot of Mr. Adamson's garden, behind his
house, were then transferred to more dignified quarters'.[4] The
collection was finally housed as the 'Museum of Antiquities' at
Newcastle University in 1954. The display of finds was a major
consideration of the excavators of South Shields whilst John Clayton's Antiquity House evolved into the Memorial Museum at the
start of the century. These museums formed a core to which addi-
tions were later made. There are now museums holding the finds of
various sites at Carlisle and Newcastle at either end of the Wall, site
museums at Corbridge, Housesteads, and Vindolanda, South Shields
and a mixture of finds at Chesters. A comparative study of these
museums is almost a time-line of museum evolution. Chesters has
already been described in Chapter Three and is, in many ways, a
fossilised remain itself. The artefacts are here largely left to speak for
themseves. Housesteads again puts the accent on the artefacts but
also attempts to tell the story of the excavations by means of wall
displays based on photographs and a short text; a scale model is also
effectively used. Vindolanda has exploited the whole panoply of
modern interpretative media and advanced technology. Reconstructions of interiors with lifesized figures combine genuine artefacts
with replicas accompanied by taped voices anachronistically speaking
fluent English. Videos tell the story of the excavations and education
officers are employed to present the site to school children. The
original wall reconstructions now include an Open Air Museum
currently consisting of, amongst other things, a Temple to the
Nymphs, a cemetery, a milestone, a shop, a Romano-British house.
They are intended as 'the reasoned reconstruction of what it once
looked like'.[5]

The overall approach to interpretation on the Wall has been fairly
slow in coming to terms with the increase in tourism following the
Second World War. Bruce and his ilk were dealing with a localised
public and writing for and speaking to a known and narrow audience
of interested non-specialists. Bruce's cult of the personality was
applicable in this context and the continuing popularity of his
Handbook reveals the effectiveness of the format. However the
ensuing academicisation of the literature of which Eric Birley's
guidebooks are an example indicate a rather blinkered approach
which ignored the implication of tourism after the War and possibly
resulted from the close identification of professional archaeology
with state control of major sites. It took the catalyst of the need to
generate money to revolutionise approaches to interpretation and

these came from the private sector with the government following a long way behind.

Notes

1. D. Lowenthal, *The Past is a Foreign Country*, Cambridge (1985), p. 249.
2. R. G. Collingwood, Preface to the Tenth edition of the *Handbook of the Roman Wall*, Newcastle-upon-Tyne (1947).
3. P. Fowler, *The Past in Contemporary Society*, London (1992), p. 137.
4. R. O. Heslop, 'The Society Museum', Centenary Edition of *Archaeologia Aeliana* (1913), p. 19.
5. R. Birley, *Report of the Friends of the Vindolanda Trust* (1994).

The Wall at Brunton. J. C. Bruce, *The Roman Wall*, 1853.

CHAPTER SIX

Defining an Ancient Monument: the Tourist Gaze

The perspective of the study so far has been that of those investigating, interpreting and, in the process, creating the monument. This chapter seeks to alter the perspective by a consideration of Hadrian's Wall from the visitor's point of view. As a focus for research with a few select visitors with a predisposition and commitment to historic remains, the monument sites no longer have the significance they once did. Organised field trips in which the excavators are there as interpreters of the sites along the model of the Pilgrimages are a rarity compared with the large numbers of 'site seers' who have increasingly overwhelmed the Wall. The rise of mass tourism, a peculiarly late-twentieth-century phenomenon, has had a profound effect on the cultural significance of the Wall as a monument in today's society. A survey of the Wall as an object to be visited has a long and entertaining history. The motives of past visitors have been varied and hopefully have some bearing on a discussion of the current state of Wall tourism.

The idea of visiting places of particular significance is an old one though the purpose has tended to change. The concept of 'the pilgrimage' as a journey to an agreed destination of religious importance was enormously popular in the medieval period and, though the motivation might now be a secular one, the basic concept still has relevance when considering attitudes to Roman antiquity in the last couple of centuries. Dr Bruce's reference to his field trips as 'Pilgrimages' had thus a resonance that was both emotional and spiritual. As a publicity coup it was quite masterful and the persistence of the Pilgrimages indicates the power of the idea. The Wall lends itself particularly well to the idea of a journey. It is something that can be 'traversed', has a definitive beginning and end, covers a variety of terrain including rocky precipices which may be 'toiled' up and verdant valleys providing rest and shelter, and has a host of local personalities to encounter on the way and the ghosts of past glories to resurrect. Bunyan and Tolkein would both have appreciated it.

The first person to have claimed to have walked the Wall was William Hutton, a Birmingham historian who wrote an account ostensibly describing the Wall's 'Ancient state and its appearance in the year 1801'.[1] This he does with much measurement and surveying and many anecdotes as to his adventures in search of food and accommodation. His description of his experience of the Wall north of Hexham conveys something of his approach: 'I climbed over a stone wall to examine the wonder; measured the whole in every direction; surveyed them with surprise, with delight, was fascinated and unable to proceed ... I had the grandest works under my eye, of the greatest men of the age in which they lived and of the most eminent nation then existing'.[2] He was less delighted by the upland area around Housesteads. 'The prospects are not grand, but extensive, and rather awful'.[3]

It is significant that Hutton walked the line; the only alternative was that taken by his daughter who went on horseback. But by this time communications were improving with the building of General Wade's road and the ending of the lawlessness of the moss troopers. The work of Clayton made accessible many more excavated remains than before and began to attract, not just antiquaries, but genuine sightseers. This coincided with the development of the railways in which Clayton was also involved. The Newcastle and Carlisle railway was available to the 1886 pilgrims and many local hotels had arrangements with the railway companies. Whereas in 1848 Bruce says 'for our mutual convenience we had an open carriage with us, and my son had his pony',[4] in 1849 the first pilgrimage used a long 'break' drawn by two horses not very imaginatively dubbed Romulus and Remus. 'My servant brought the luncheon from Newcastle in my phaeton'.[5]

Hadrian's Wall does not seem to have figured greatly on the set

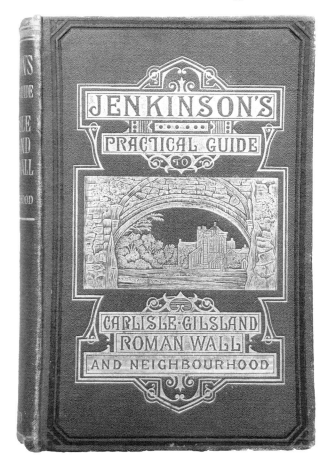

FIGURE 24.
Jenkinson's
Practical Guide
1875.

tourist route of the eighteenth century, being overshadowed by the much vaunted beauties of the Lake District. *Jenkinson's Practical Guide* of 1875 refers to the area as being little known although traversed by the railway. It gives advice on access to sites and general descriptions. At Housesteads 'the situation is wild and solitary, but the ruins are so extensive and give evidence of such massiveness and grandeur, that the stranger, when wandering alone amongst the scattered broken columns, will feel that he is in a city of the dead, and he will be reminded of Pompeii or Babylon, or of Scipio amongst the ruins of Carthage'.[6]

A picture of the tourist experience on the Wall through the eyes of a non-antiquarian is found in Maria A. Hoyer's description of her summer holiday in 1908. She arrived at Chollerford 'by a train that trotted about the countryside, apparently intent on paying morning calls at little stations where nobody got in and fewer got out'.[7] Her visit to Chesters was a tour in the company of other visitors conducted by Thomas Tailford, John Clayton's foreman in the days of his excavations, who spoke of his discoveries displayed in the museum. Access to Housesteads was facilitated by organising an excursion for a group of guests from the George Hotel travelling not in the expected wagonette but a landeau with liveried coachman. She compares Chesters rather unfavourably with Housesteads referring to Chesters' 'order and tidiness', the 'proximity of the modern mansion and its well-cared for grounds, the coming and going of the tourists, detract from its visionary force'.[8] At Housesteads it is easier to 'sit and dream, to send ones spirit into the past ... slowly and dimly the grey ruined walls rise and are capped with battlements as the great camp stands square to the wintry wind'.[9] At Corstopitum she is a witness to the excavations where

> a noticeboard informed all whom it might concern that non-subscribers could see the exavations on payment of sixpence ... men were at work digging trenches recklessly amid the yellow grain. The ground was further ornamented with little flags of different colours on short sticks stuck about the field.[10]

Her reference to a young man in charge who showed her the sculptured figure of a lion crouching on the back of a stag recently excavated was probably Leonard Woolley.[11]

A. G. Bradley visited the Wall two years later and speaks of meeting only eight people whilst walking in the central sector in August. He too meets the 'veteran', Tailford mentioning that Chesters is open one day in the week on which about 50 people usually are attracted

FIGURE 25. "Roman Lion, Corbridge". Postcard produced by Gibson & Son. Reproduced by permission of Northumberland Record Office.

'pilgrims mainly from the outer world, an intelligent and interested company as I saw them for the most part'.[12] His assessment of the Wall's central sector echoes Maria Hoyer; to the north it 'stretches in undulating solitude, as profound in every essential as when the shivering sentinels of the Roman watch towers scanned it for the irrepressible barbarian'.[13]

Hutton was Jessie Mothersole's inspiration for her rather madcap traverse of the Wall, an account of which she published in 1922. She had attended the 1920 Pilgrimage and being 'an artist with a taste for archaeology'[14] had walked the Wall, illustrating it en-route. A large portion of this work is a panegyric on Governor Agricola and is written in a rather breathless present tense including a description of her reaction to her approach to the Wall's central sector, 'now goodbye to the high road and hurrah for the heights'.[15]

In *In Search of England*, published in 1927 (and going into twenty editions), H. V. Morton was inspired to hold a conversation with an imaginary centurion on the subject of the weather. 'It still comes down like Hades, does it?' he would ask ... 'I suppose you had duck boards; and did they send you mouth organs and woolies from Rome?',[16] and so on.

Hutton's truest imitator was perhaps Hunter Davies who published his *A Walk Along the Wall* in 1974. It is still in print today. Like Hutton's, his is an account as much of the social condition of the area as it is today as a reflection on the monument itself. This book had wide circulation, later being published in paperback. Davies at the time was a popular and high profile commentator and journalist and his book was serialised in the press. He gives a vivid picture of the Wall at the height of its popularity. 'Hadrian's Wall is a living wall, not just for the local inhabitants but for tourists and archaeologists, a living, breathing, expanding, growing wall'.[17]

As these examples of tourist literature demonstrate, being a tourist is a state of mind, a state that involves preconceptions fed by images and certain inculcated ways of looking and seeing. What the tourist chooses to visit and his or her response to the object of the visit is very much a matter of taste. Ian Ousby has defined taste as 'the application of general tendencies of thought and cultural attitude to the act of judging one aspect of our environment as interesting, beautiful, or otherwise worth attention and rejecting others as not'.[18] The tourist literature of the Wall effectively illustrates different aspects of taste arising from the reactions inspired by its complex integration of monument and scenery.

Two aspects of this literature are particularly noticeable. Firstly the impact of Romanticism on visitors' responses is profound, though not necessarily something of which the writers were consciously aware. Apart from Hutton who was a pre-Romantic figure, reactions to the wild and lonely scenery of Housesteads and its environs are predictably ecstatic, the cultivated and manicured sites of Chesters and Corbridge less so. The second aspect, an off-shoot of the first, is the evocative response to the Wall. It inspires a need to conjure up the past in the imagination, a need based more on

FIGURE 26.
Illustration from
J. C. Bruce, *The
Handbook to the
Roman Wall*, 1914.

atmosphere than on hard historical fact. Visitors, such as Maria Hoyer, invariably find the remains a cause for reflection on the passage of time and the possibility of empathy between themselves and the people originally creating and inhabiting what is now decay and dereliction. Hadrian's Wall is the ultimate 'Ruin in a Land-scape'[19] on a par with Tintern Abbey and the other inspirations of the Romantic movement. It has the truly 'picturesque' quality of a ruin in an imposing landscape reverting to Nature in an uncontrived manner. It fulfills the dictats by arbiters of taste such as John Gilpin who wrote very early proto-guide books which defined picturesque beauty in the mid-eighteenth century.

A later reverence for Nature and the landscape, inspired by William Wordsworth, revolutionised people's way of viewing scenery and greatly influenced contemporary tourist literature. This is demonstrated in Jenkinson's guide and the later work of Hoyer and Bradley, 'Guidebooks no longer abbreviated the region (the Lake District) to a series of selective views; ... they radiated the new seriousness of purpose appropriate to a culture which sought nature out, not as a source for cultivated amusement, but as an educational and, indeed, a religious experience'.[20] Visiting monuments is seen as an uplifting experience, maybe even the secular equivalent of the religious pilgrimage.

Wordsworth's influence arose from his interest in the Lake District; however, there were other literary figures more closely associated with the area around the Wall. Sir Walter Scott, a major trend-setter of the Romantic movement, set a number of his novels in Hadrian's Wall's vicinity and his popular *Border Antiquities* published in 1817 gave an account of castles, abbeys and the like, dating from the Roman

FIGURE 27.
Illustration from J. C. Bruce, *The Handbook to the Roman Wall*, 1914.

period to his own day. He was not by inclination drawn to the Roman period with its classical associations, preferring the Gothic; however, he did write a poem entitled 'To a Lady, with Flowers from the Roman Wall, 1797' which is both Romantic and evocative:

> *Take these flowers which, purple waving,*
> *On the ruin'd rampart grew,*
> *Where the sons of freedom braving,*
> *Rome's imperial standards flew.*
> *Warriors from the breach of danger*
> *Pluck no longer laurels there;*
> *They but yield the passing stranger*
> *Wild-flower wreaths for Beauty's hair.*

This 'retrospective nostalgia for a lost, irretrievable past'[21] is at variance with many aspects of the antiquarian point of view. Stuart Piggott has traced 'two parallel strands of antiquarianism',[22] namely the new Romanticism promoted by Scott which appealed particularly to tourist and guidebook writers, and the 'revived empiricism' which was a feature of Clayton's and the fellow members of the Newcastle Society's approach with its accent on excavation and the collecting, minute recording and cataloguing of the resulting antiquities. The purpose of these investigations Lowenthal would see in 'neo-classical' terms, 'an attempt to reconstruct remote glories in the service of modern progress'[23] rather than reflect on the transience of the human condition as symbolised by the traces it leaves behind. Bruce, for instance, in his preface to the *Handbook* sees 'the benefit of tracing Roman 'memorials' as an opportunity to 'hold fellowship

FIGURE 28.
Illustration from
J. C. Bruce, *The Handbook to the Roman Wall*, 1914.

FIGURE 29. "Murus Fosse, Limestone Bank". Postcard produced by Gibson & Son. Reproduced by permission of Northumberland Record Office.

with the mighty men of the past' hence 'inbibing some of their courage and some of their lofty aspirations.'[24]

There are, perhaps, parallel traces of Romanticism in some of the pictorial images of the Wall. Majestic scenery and overgrown ruins overwhelming diminutive figures are a frequent feature of the Richardson watercolours and lithographs. Many of the illustrations in early editions of the Handbook, if not by the Richardsons, are inspired by them and have similar picturesque themes. Rather than the regulatory passing shepherd or hermit the figures tend to be aristocratic-looking gentlemen but the proportions are still the same.

More surprisingly, in a medium more geared to a documentary approach, some of the work of J. P. Gibson also has the hallmark of the Romantic. His work can be both documentary and artistic reflecting, in Piggott's terms both the 'empirical' and 'romantic'. Sometimes the two merge; his postcard view of Chesterholm is a record of the site in which the milestone is carefully kept in view to the left, but the picture as a whole also has a brooding quality. His landscape view of the river Irthing from Birdoswald is immaculately composed and carefully framed whilst his view of Housesteads 'Pretorium' works equally well as a record and an accomplished

FIGURE 30. "Chesterholme". Postcard produced by Gibson & Son. Reproduced by permission of Northumberland Record Office.

FIGURE 31. "Pretorium Housesteads". Postcard produced by Gibson & Son. Reproduced by permission of Northumberland Record Office.

landscape. The requisite decorative figure appears in his 'murus fosse' at Limestone corner.

The 'neo-classical' is evident in the prosaically titled 'Building of the Roman Wall' painted as one of a series representing Northumbrian history by William Bell in 1850. It is unmistakably located on Hotbank Crags with Crag Lough in the background; the rest is imaginative reconstruction with the accent on 'imaginative'. According to Jim Crow, 'The Roman Officer was modelled on John Clayton. At his feet, the sharp profile of John Collingwood Bruce looks towards the hostile natives'.[25] He is accompanied by a Victorian lady whose presence on the scene is hard to fathom. 'Night Attack' by Robert Spence of 1914 is also rather unfathomable, not to say gloomy,

FIGURE 32. "Night Attack" by Robert Spence, 1914. Reproduced by permission of Museum of Antiquities.

and historically even more unlikely. It purports to depict an assault on Housesteads Fort via the North Gate and is thought to have been at first conceived as a day attack, but the concept was changed in the course of painting.

The Wall set in a landscape dominated by the Whin Sill is a powerful and recurrent image which continues to inspire photographers, painters, poets and novelists. Amongst writers, Scott has already been mentioned; a later writer of undoubted influence as an image maker was Rudyard Kipling. In *Puck of Pooks Hill*, published in 1906, unlike Scott, he sets his stories securely in a fictional Roman past in which the Wall figures not as a ruin but a living, functioning edifice, a symbol of Roman power. His description of Parnesius' first sight of the Wall is an intensely powerful evocation written by someone with direct experience of the landscape.

> Just when you think you are at the world's end, you see a smoke from east to west as far as the eye can turn and then ... houses and temples, shops and theatres, barracks and granaries, trickling along like dice behind – always behind – one long, low, rising and falling, and hiding and showing line of towers. And that is the Wall.[26]

Kipling's interest in the Wall is testified to in his letter to *The Times* (see Chapter 4). Jessie Mothersole's account of her tour of the Wall refers to the visitors' book at the George Hotel, Chollerford, which was the accustomed base for Wall visitors, as containing the signatures of both Kipling and Bernard Shaw. The stories in *Puck of Pook's Hill* were written at a time when Kipling was at the height of his fame and they must have been widely read by both adults and children.

Thus the tourist view was not necessarily an open-minded, objective reaction to a monument in a certain landscape on a certain day, but an amalgam of literary and pictorial representations creating certain preconceptions and expectations both conscious and unconscious.

Notes

1. William Hutton, *The History of the Roman Wall*, 1813 (Reprinted 1990), Newcastle, title page.
2. *Ibid*, p. 3.
3. *Ibid*, p. 64.
4. J. C. Bruce, *Proceedings of the Society of Antiquaries of Newcastle*, Vol. 2 (1886), p. 136.
5. *Ibid*.

6. H. I. Jenkinson, *Jenkinson's Practical Guides, Carlisle to Gilsland, Roman Wall and Neighbourhood*, London (1875) p. 203.

7. Maria A. Hoyer, *By the Roman Wall, Notes on a Summer Holiday*, London (1908).

8. *Ibid*, p. 23.

9. *Ibid*, p. 24.

10. *Ibid*, p. 84.

10. M. C. Bishop, *Corstopitum, An Edwardian Excavation*, English Heritage (1994), p. 45.

12. A. G. Bradley, *The Romance of Northumberland*, London (1908), p. 220.

13. *Ibid*, p. 233.

14. Jessie Mothersole, *Hadrian's Wall*, London (1922), p. 24.

15. Ibid, p. 109.

16. H. V. Morton, *In Search of England*, London (1927), p. 198.

17. Hunter Davies, *A Walk Along the Wall*, 1974, p. 155.

18. Ian Ousby, *The Englishman's England, Taste, Travel and the Rise of Tourism*, Cambridge (1990), p. 5.

19. Stuart Piggott, *Ruins in a Landscape, Essays in Antiquarianism*, Edinburgh (1976).

20. Ousby, *Op. cit.*, p. 179.

21. D. Lowenthal, *The Past is a Foreign Country*, Cambridge (1985), p. 181.

22. Piggott, *Op. cit.*, p. 134.

23. Lowenthal, *Op. cit.*, p. 181.

24. J. C. Bruce, *Handbook to the Roman Wall*, Newcastle (1884), Preface.

25. J. Crow, *Housesteads*, London (1995), Plate 10.

26. Rudyard Kipling, *Puck of Pook's Hill*, London (1906), p. 135.

CHAPTER SEVEN

Conclusion:
Whose Wall is it Anyway?

The bulk of this book was originally written as a dissertation for a master's degree submitted in 1995. As the author's offering landed on the doormat of Lancaster University's History Department, English Heritage was consulting on its Draft Management Plan for the Hadrian's Wall World Heritage Site. The final plan was published in 1996 since when the designation of the Wall has begun to have a significant impact and much has been happening in 'Hadrian's Wall Country'. An archaeological park situated in an area desperately needing some urban regeneration at Wallsend is being set up. This so far includes a re-constructed section of the wall, the displayed remains of the fort of Segendum and the reconstruction of a working bathhouse. The bathhouse has recently been fired for the first time and should provide the ultimate in authentic Roman bathing experiences are just a few instances. Vindolanda has gone from strength to strength and Robin Birley and his son, Andrew, have excavated on the site of the stone fort in conjunction with English Heritage. The promotion of the heritage site as a whole is now being co-ordinated by the Hadrian's Wall Tourism Partnership and some important issues of interpretation for visitors are being imaginatively addressed and systematically researched. The Wall now has its own full time 'One Man Roman Army', Jeff Barnett, affectionately known as 'Jefficus'. Tour-guides are for the first time being recruited and trained by the Tourism Partnership. The Wall has its own web-site.

The implications of this study for the future of the Wall as a monument, however, even after five years, on the whole remain the same. English Heritage's Draft Management Plan has a chapter entitled 'A Vision for Hadrian's Wall'.[1] The attempt to come to terms with the enormous complexity of the monument and to establish some coherent view of the future of the Wall might be considered long overdue. The context in which the Plan establishes its proposals echoes much that has been discussed in this work.

A co-ordinated approach to the management of the Wall is obviously desirable. However the haphazard nature of its development has created an inheritance in which there is much confusion, potential conflict of interest and ambiguity. The recurrent question underlying the whole debate should be that of its ideological owner-ship i.e. Who is the Wall for? This begs the question of what institution should own and can best safeguard the Wall in the interests of the innumerable groups and individuals for whom it has particular significance.

The plan identifies the academic community's interests by express-ing the need for 'an agreed academic framework for research on Hadrian's Wall'.[2] It does not however make the connection between such research and another of its identified interests, those of the 'lay' visitor. Improved interpretation is seen as desirable 'to deliver a high quality visitor experience'.[3] Good interpretation however requires accessible archaeological information and this is not always easily attainable under current circumstances. The Royal Commission's National Monuments Record constitutes the main archive which is a vast and technically complex database. The need for a specific Hadrian's Wall database which would be the foundation for a coher-ent research strategy for the Wall was recognised in the Management Plan but has yet to be achieved. Once established, it would then hopefully feed into a coherent approach to the interpretation of the whole Wall.

The commitment to making archaeological knowledge accessible to the public should be seen, perhaps, as a vital part of future planning. The legacy of popular archaeology exemplified by Bruce, although needing reinterpretation in the context of mass tourism, should not be lost amongst the professional preoccupations of university archaeology departments and archaeology units and in the corridors of power at English Heritage. 'Archaeology is a creative pursuit, rather like theatre it depends upon its public'.[4]

The contribution made to the popularisation of the archaeology of the Wall by local rather than national institutions has been a feature of this study. The contribution of antiquarian and archaeo-logical societies of the area to the developing understanding of the monument has historically been of great significance. Their gradual marginalisation, outlined in previous chapters, has resulted in the neglect of a useful resource. It might be part of the role of the Co-ordination Unit to encourage the participation of amateur so-cieties in areas such as research, excavation and conservation. There should be room for both amateurs and professionals in the conser-vation and further investigation of the Wall. If research is to avoid becoming remote from those concerned with the Wall in its fullest sense as monument with complex associations which are cultural and social as well as academic, it needs to cultivate those with a non-specialist interest in the best antiquarian tradition.

In mitigation of this concern it should be noted that from 14th to 21st August, 1999 there occurred an event redolent with past antiquarian glories. The Twelfth Pilgrimage of Hadrian's Wall took place, organised in the traditional manner by the two sister societies concerned with Hadrian's Wall, The Cumberland and Westmorland Antiquarian and Archaeological Society and the Society of Antiquaries of Newcastle upon Tyne. This must be an event unique in world archaeology and witness to the continuing self-awareness of the profession's origins and the significance of the Wall in its development. In the 'Summary of Recent Excavations and Research', the handbook traditionally prepared for the pilgrims, Paul Bidwell refers to the Pilgrimages as 'acts of veneration for the best- known Roman monument in Britain'.[5] A sense of history pervaded the proceedings commencing with the laying of a wreath on the tomb of J. Collingwood Bruce by Professor David Breeze much of whose career has been involved in unravelling the mysteries of the Wall. The popularity of the pilgrimage bears witness to its continuing function as a social occasion which provides a public opportunity to publicise the wealth and quality of scholarship which continues to make the

FIGURE 33. Pilgrimage, 1999. Willowford Bridge. Reproduced by permission of B. J. N. Edwards.

Roman frontier in Britain one of the best researched monuments of its type in the world.

The fact remains that the Pilgrimage only happens once in ten years and is severely restricted in the numbers it can involve and many of these are professional archaeologists.

A possible role model for the continuing participation of a local community is to be found in the site of South Shields where the local associations of an earlier era have been capitalised upon. It has its own archaeology unit working in conjunction with a museum's service and a carefully fostered amateur archaeological society, the Arbeia Society. It has a long history of amateur excavations and continues to encourage these under professional supervision. The Management Plan places great emphasis on the importance of developing such urban sites as a means of deflecting visitor pressure from more scenic sites. This strategy neglects their significance as foci for local communities based on a pride in and concern for their Roman Remains. Visitors and tourists are not necessarily the same thing.

Two interests have been discussed so far, the amateur and professional. A third, that of the tourist, tends to take precedence in The Management Plan. Tourism is where the money comes from and the early setting-up and financing of the Hadrian's Wall Tourism Partnership under the auspices of the Co-ordination Unit set up by English Heritage to implement the management plan bears witness to the importance placed upon the promotion of tourism. The Wall in this context might be seen as a product to be packaged and marketed; however, it does also have to concern itself with problems of conservation. Two radically opposed concepts are entailed here. The paradox of tourism as a general phenomenon is that it destroys that which it comes to see. Whilst conservation has been a continuing theme from the antiquarian period, the problem of the destruction of the wall as a result of easy access by car is a relatively new phenomenon, reaching a climax in the 1970s. An attempt to resolve this dilemma has been put forward in the idea of 'green tourism' and the education of visitors into an awareness of the fragility of what they see. The Management Plan addresses this dilemma although its resolution will be much more difficult than a statement of the problem. There still remains potential conflict in the promotion of certain sites out of economic considerations and the protection of the national heritage.

Promotion involves the effective interpretation of the Wall. As has been outlined already, site ownership has had an effect on the approaches taken. The case of Vindolanda has been used to exemplify the approach of private enterprise. Robin Birley has been more concerned with the excavation of the site than with its conservation whereas for English Heritage and its preceeding government bodies conservation has tended to take precedence. In Robin Birley's words, 'We've done 25 years full time work on this site and there's at least 200 years more here'.[6] His excavations are directly financed by income from visitors and, in order to generate that income, he has chosen to interpret the site in a sophisticated manner already described in chapters three and six. Unlike state controlled sites he has been in a position in which, by excavation, he can create the product and subsequently interpret and sell it. The evolution of the site along 'theme park' lines raises questions about the nature of visitors' experience as discussed in Chapter Six.

The recent re-constructions on the site at Wallsend initiated by the same team as those responsible for the South Shields gate reconstruction may also raise theme park issues however the justification may lie with the urban nature of the site. This is located in the midst of an industrial scene of advanced dereliction in which the opportunity to experience a Roman bath in a reconstructed bathhouse seems a suitable and original means of promoting a local interest in Roman history where it might not have previously been inspired.

One site, though not discussed in previous chapters, deserves mention here as a pioneer in many fields over the past few years. The site at the fort of Birdoswald in the central wall sector has been adopting new approaches and has been in the vanguard of both research and interpretation in recent years. The roots of its success may lie in the atypical nature of its funding and administration. In 1984 the farm and land on which the fort lies was bought by Cumbria County Council as a resource for tourists and for educational use. It also obtained the funding of private enterprise in the form of British Nuclear Fuels. Their money enabled new archaeological research to be undertaken in the form of an unusually extensive excavation of a previously unexcavated and little known areas of the fort adjoining the farmhouse. The results of these excavations placed Birdoswald at the cutting edge of wall research, particularly of the later period of Roman occupation. The fate of the Wall at the end of the occupation and into the Dark Ages was little understood partly because much was often ignored and destroyed in the fervour of nineteenth- and early twentieth-century 'wall chasing'. There is a close relationship between the archaeological research and carefully constructed on-site interpretation. This is achieved in the form of a visitor centre and exhibition, an excellent written guide plus the services of site-based tour guides. Visitors are provided with an enlightening experience designed to develop their understanding of the processes and history of archaeology along side their awareness of the Wall as part of Roman history. Independent finance has provided opportunities for the professional management and promotion of the site and this has contributed greatly to its success. A residential study centre has recently been developed on the site with the aid of Lottery funding. This felicitous amalgam of local authority, private enterprise and the archaeological expertise of English Heritage is, perhaps, a pointer to the future development of other sites.

On a more philosophical note, it has hopefully been demonstrated in the course of this study that responses to such a monument as Hadrian's Wall are complicated and often emotional. Firstly, responses involve an interest in the remains as evidence of the past set in a certain historical period and to understand them in any meaningful way some explanation is required. Visitors also respond to a certain atmosphere created by the setting of the remains and by expectations based on pre-existing images. The preconception visitors have of monuments is an area of research only touched on here. The stereotype of the 'lonely roman soldier' enduring wind and rain clad in sandals and a mini-skirt, and writing forlorn letters home to Rome is an enduring one and it must be the purpose of good interpretation to restructure such preconceptions. The means by which this may be done are becoming more and more elaborate in an era of virtual reality and 'live' re-enactments. Within the constraints of current archaeological knowledge, the past can in some respects be recreated in the present. The fact still remains however that the 'past is a foreign country'.[7] The past is different from the present and it is misleading to indicate that the thoughts, attitudes and spiritual aspirations of past people can be recaptured. Monuments, by their nature, require an imaginative response on the part of the visitor, an attempt at evocation peculiar to that person and requiring an active, imaginative involvement rather than passive acceptance of the interpretation. The remains are symbols of a distant past subject themselves to the passage of time. This 'Romantic' approach is an aspect of the Wall's cultural history that is in danger of being lost in an era of mass tourism and its associated heritage industry. Though there is no denying the place of interpretation in the provision of a meaningful visitor experience, a monument is essentially a 'reminder' of a distant past, not a representation of the past itself and should be cherished as such.

This is, in itself, admittedly, a 'Romantic' point of view in the sense of being unrealistic. The antiquaries and visitors of the last century and the beginning of this were privileged in their access to such a remote and beautiful place as the central sector of the Wall. It is difficult for the modern day visitor to contemplate his or her own mortality at Housesteads on a Bank Holiday but I would like to think it not impossible.

In designating Hadrian's Wall as a World Heritage Site the intention has not been to change it in any fundamental way but to raise a general awareness of its importance. The Management Plan's 'guiding principle' for the Wall is declared to be to 'Keep things as they are, or better'.[8] The balance between maintaining the preserved remains as an inheritance to be handed on to future generations and creating a sterile and fossilised structure packaged merely as a tourist attraction is a fine one. Without the continuation of the research into the 'problem' of the Wall, without the perpetual struggle to explain the enigma of the Wall, its dynamism and meaning will be lost along with any real social and cultural significance.

'He who contemplates a pilgrimage *per lineam Valli*, if he be imbued with a thorough love of antiquity, and duly appreciate the importance of the great structure which invites his attention, will not lightly enter upon the enterprise'.[9] Neither should the enterprise of writing a history of Hadrian's Wall be 'lightly entered upon'. This study has chosen to raise a few of the numerous issues implicit in such a wide-ranging subject and has inevitably failed to analyse many of the themes in the depth they deserve. Hopefully the opportunity will arise for further research on the basis of a dialogue with those currently concerned with Hadrian's Wall in all its many facets. The final hope might be that the new vision for the Wall will ensure that pilgrims such as the present writer who, at the age of seventeen, first walked the Wall, Dr Bruce's Handbook at the ready, will always be enabled to continue on their journey.

Notes

1. English Heritage, *Hadrian's Wall Military Zone, Draft Management Plan* (1995).
2. *Ibid*, p. 11.
3. *Ibid*, p. 50.

4. B. Cunliffe, *The Public Face of the Past, Antiquity and Man – Essays in Honour of Glynn Daniel*, London (1981), p. 192.

5. P. T. Bidwell, *Hadrian's Wall, 1989–1999*, Carlisle (1999), p. 4.

6. B. Houghton, *Tangle in the Wall Zone*, Heritage Today (Sept. 1994).

7. L. P. Hartley, *The Go-Between* quoted in D. Lowenthal, The Past is a Foreign Country, London (1985).

8. English Heritage, *op. cit.*, p. 12.

9. J. C. Bruce, *Handbook to The Roman Wall*, Newcastle (1914), p. 2.

Bibliography

Abbreviation

AA   *Archaeologia Aeliana* (Journal of Society of Antiquaries of Newcastle)

Primary Sources

Books

E. Birley, *Book of the Centenary Pilgrimage of Hadrian's Wall, 4th July–9th July, 1949*.

E. Birley, Introduction to J. Hodgson, *History of Northumberland*, Vol. 4 (1840) Reprint 1974.

J. C. Bruce, *The Roman Wall*, Newcastle (1853).

J. C. Bruce, *Handbook to the Roman Wall*, Newcastle (1914).

Ibid. Ed. R. G. Collingwood (1947).

A. G. Bradley, *The Romance of Northumberland*, London (1908).

E. A. Wallis Budge, *An Account of the Roman Antiquities Preserved in the Museum at Chesters, Northumberland*, London (1907).

R. G. Collingwood, *An Autobiography*, London (1939).

H. Davies, *A Walk Along the Wall*, London (1974).

C. Daniels, *The Eleventh Pilgrimage of Hadrian's Wall*, Newcastle (1989).

R. Embleton and F. Graham, *Hadrian's Wall in the Days of the Romans*, Newcastle (1984).

M. A. Hoyer, *By the Roman Wall, Notes on a Summer Holiday*, London (1908).

W. Hutton, *The History of the Roman Wall*, London (1813).

R. Kipling, *Puck of Pook's Hill*, London (1906).

H. V. Morton, *In Search of England*, London (1927).

J. Mothersole, *Hadrian's Wall*, London (1922).

H. R. Robinson, *What the Soldiers Wore on Hadrian's Wall*, Newcastle (1976).

R. Welford, *Men of Mark Twixt Tyne and Tees*, London (1895).

Manuscripts and Photographs

R. Birley, *Friends of Vindolanda Trust Report* (1994).

R. Birley, *Profile of the Vindolanda Trust*.

R. Blair, *Collectiana* (1957), Collection of South Shields Public Library.

The North of England Excavation Committee Accounts 1925–1935 (Hadrian's Wall Collection, Museum of Antiquities of the University and Society of Antiquaries of Newcastle upon Tyne, Newcastle).

Photographs, Hadrian's Wall Archive, Museum of Antiquities of the University and Society of Antiquaries of Newcastle upon Tyne.

Photographs of South Shields Roman Fort, South Shields Public Library Collection.

Gibson Collection, Northumberland Public Record Office.

Press cuttings, South Shields Roman Fort, Archaeology Unit.

Official Reports and Guidebooks

Ash Consulting Group, *A Sustainable Tourism Marketing Strategy for the Hadrian's Wall/Tyne Valley Corridor* (1994).

E. Birley, *Chesters Roman Fort Official Guidebook*, London,(1960).

E. Birley, *Corstopitum Roman Fort Official Guidebook*, London, Various editions.

English Heritage, *Draft Management Plan, Hadrian's Wall Military Zone* (1995).

J. G. Crow and A. Rushworth, *Housesteads Roman Fort and its Environs*, English Heritage (1994).

Dartington Amenity Trust, *Hadrian's Wall – A Strategy for Conservation and Visitor Services*, Dart Publication No. 25 (1976).

R. M. Guard, *John Pattison Gibson, 1838–1912*, Northumberland Record Office (1982).

Hadrian's Wall Consultative Committee, *The Strategy for Hadrian's Wall*, Newcastle (1984).

H. I. Jenkinson, *Jenkinson's Practical Guide to Carlisle, Gilsland, Roman Wall and Neighbourhood*, London (1875).

R. Woodside, *The National Trust Archaeology Survey, Hadrian's Wall Estate*, Vol. 1 (1995).

Proceedings of the Cumberland and Westmorland Antiquarian and Archaeological Society, Reports on the Pilgrimages of 1920, 1930, 1949 and 1959 in Transactions, N.S., Vols XXI, XXXI, V, VX.

Tyne and Wear Museums Service, The Roman Fort of Arbeia at South Shields (1993).

Articles

R. Birley, 'Hadrian's Wall 1970–1982', *Popular Archaeology*, Vol. 4, No. 11 (1983), pp. 2–3.

J. C. Bruce, *Proceedings of the Society of Antiquaries of Newcastle upon Tyne*, Vol. 2 (1886), p. 136.

R. G. Collingwood, 'Hadrian's Wall : A History of the Problem', *Journal of Roman Studies*, XI (1921), pp. 37–66.

R. E. Hoopell, 'On the Discovery and Exploration of the Roman Remains at South Shields in the year 1875–6', *Transactions of the Natural History Society of Northumberland, Durham and Newcastle*, Vol. VIII (1878), pp. 126–167.

R. Birley, *Report of the Friends of the Vindolanda Trust* (1994).

Newspapers

Shields Gazette, 20 February 1875 and 22 March 1875.

Newcastle Journal, 30 November 1984.

The Times, 23 April 1974 and 15 July 1949.

Secondary Sources

Articles

E. Birley, 'Excavations at Corstopitum 1906–1958', *AA4*, XXXVII (1959), pp. 1–31.

R. C. Bosanquet, 'J. Lingard, Notes Transcribed and Annotated', *AA4*, VI (1929) pp. 130–162.

R. O. Heslop, 'The Society Museum', *AA Centenary Volume* (1913), pp. 13–25.

T. Hodgkin, 'John Collingwood Bruce', *AA2* XV (1892), p. 368.

G. Jobey, 'The Society of Antiquaries of Newcastle on Tyne', *AA5*, XVIII (1990), pp. 197–216.

W. Lawson, 'The Construction of the Military Road in Northumberland 1745–1757', *AA5*, II (1973), pp. 177–193.

I. A. Richmond, 'The Roman Fort at South Shields', *AA4*, XI (1934), pp. 83–103.

I. A. Richmond, 'F. G. Simpson', *AA4*, XXXIV (1956), pp. 219–221.

G. Sumner, 'Illustrating Archaeology, Pictures of the Past', *Popular Archaeology*, Vol. 4, No. 7 (1983), p. 13–19.

R. Welford and J. Hodgson, , 'John Clayton', *AA Centenary Volume* (1913), pp. 182–185.

Books

R. Bellhouse, *Hadrian's Wall, 1886: The Beginning of an Era*, Ledbury (1980).

P. T. Bidwell, *Hadrian's Wall, 1989–1999*, Carlisle (1999).

E. Birley, *Research on Hadrian's Wall*, Kendal (1961).

R. Birley, *The Making of Modern Vindolanda with the Life and Work of Anthony Hedley 1777–1835*, Greeenhead (1995).

R. Birley, *Vindolanda, A Roman Frontier Post on Hadrian's Wall*, London (1977).

M. C. Bishop, *Corstopitum, An Edwardian Excavation*, English Heritage (1994).

C. Chippindale, *Stonehenge Complete*, London (1983).

J. Crow, *Housesteads*, London (1995).

G. Daniel, *150 Years of Archaeology*, London (1975).

J. Evans, *A History of the Society of Antiquaries*, Oxford (1956).

J. Evans, B. Cunliffe, C. Renfrew (eds), *Antiquity and Man Essays in Honour of Glyn Daniel*, London (1981).

P. Fowler, *The Past in Contemporary Society*, London (1992).

K. Hudson, *A Social History of Archaeology*, London (1981).

S. Johnson, *Hadrian's Wall*, London (1989).

P. Levine, *The Amateur and the Professional*, Cambridge (1986).

D. Lowenthal, *The Past is a Foreign Country*, Cambridge (1985).

D. Lowenthal and M. Binney (ed.), *Our Past Before Us. Why Do We Save It?* London (1981).

E. Moir, *The Discovery of Britain : The English Tourists*, London (1964).

I. Ousby, *The Englishman's England, Taste, Travel and the Rise of Tourism*, Cambridge (1990).

S. Piggott, *William Stukeley*, Oxford (1950).

S. Piggott, *Ruins in a Landscape, Essays in Antiquarianism*, Edinburgh (1976).

S. Piggott, *Approach to Archaeology*, London (1959).

Index

Occasional Papers from the Centre for North-West Regional Studies

The Centre for North-West Regional Studies, based at Lancaster University, brings together members of the university and the regional community. As well as its extensive publication programme of books and resource papers, it organises conferences, study days and seminars covering a wide range of subjects. For a small annual subscription 'Friends of the Centre' receive regular mailings of events and discounts on books and other activities.

For further details contact Centre for North-West Regional Studies, Fylde College, Lancaster University, Lancaster, LA1 4YF; tel: 01524 593770; fax: 01524 594725; email: christine.wilkinson@lancaster.ac.uk; Web site: www.lancs.ac.uk/users/cnwrs.

Hadrian's Wall: A Social and Cultural History, 2000, Alison Ewin	£8.50
Furness Abbey: Romance, Scholarship and Culture, 2000, C. Dade-Robertson	£11.50
Rural Industries of the Lune Valley, 2000, ed. Michael Winstanley	£9.95
The Romans at Ribchester, 2000, B. J. N. Edwards	£8.95
The Buildings of Georgian Lancaster, (revised edition), 2000, Andrew White	£6.95
A History of Linen in the North West, 1998, ed. Elizabeth Roberts	£6.95
History of Catholicism in the Furness Peninsula 1127–1997, 1998, Anne C. Parkinson	£6.95
Vikings in North-West England – The Artifacts, 1998, B. J. N. Edwards	£6.95
Sharpe, Paley and Austin, A Lancaster Architectural Practice 1836–1942, 1998, James Price	£6.95
Romans and Britons in North-West England, (revised edition), 1997, David Shotter	£6.95
Victorian Terraced Houses in Lancaster, 1996, Andrew White and Michael Winstanley	£6.95
Walking Roman Roads in the Fylde and the Ribble Valley, 1996, Philip Graystone	£5.95
Romans in Lunesdale, 1995, David Shotter and Andrew White	£6.50
Roman Route Across the Northern Lake District, 1994, Martin Allan	£5.95
Walking Roman Roads in East Cumbria, 1994, Philip Graystone	£5.95
St Martin's College, Lancaster, 1964–89, 1993, Peter S. Gedge and Lois M. R. Louden	£5.95
Lydia Becker and the Cause, 1992, Audrey Kelly	£5.95
From Lancaster to the Lakes: the Region in Literature, 1992, eds Keith Hanley and Alison Millbank	£5.95
Walking Roman Roads in Bowland, 1992, Philip Graystone	£5.50
Windermere in the Nineteenth Century, 1991, ed. Oliver M. Westall	£4.95
A Traditional Grocer: T. D. Smith's of Lancaster 1858–1981, 1991, ed. Michael Winstanley	£4.95
The Roman Fort and Town of Lancaster, 1990, David Shotter and Andrew White	£4.95
Grand Fashionable Nights: Kendal Theatre, 1989, Margaret Eddershaw	£3.95
Rural Life in South West Lancashire, 1988, Alistair Mutch	£3.95
The Diary of William Fisher of Barrow, 1986, eds William Rollinson and Brett Harrison	£2.95
Popular Leisure and the Music Hall in 19th-Century Bolton, 1982, Robert Poole	£2.95
Richard Marsden and the Preston Chartists, 1981, J. E. King	£2.95

Each of these titles may be ordered by post from the above address, postage and packing £1.00 per order. Please make cheques payable to 'The University of Lancaster'. Titles are also available from all good booksellers in the region.